Women Warriors

of the Afro-Latina Diaspora

Edited by

Marta Moreno Vega

Marinieves Alba

Yvette Modestin

Arte Público Press
Houston, Texas

Women Warriors of the Afro-Latina Diaspora is made possible through a grant from the city of Houston through the Houston Arts Alliance.

Recovering the past, creating the future

Arte Público Press
University of Houston
4902 Gulf Fwy, Bldg 19, Rm 100
Houston, Texas 77204-2004

Cover design by James F. Brisson
Cover art by Yasmin Hernandez (*Ayi lo da,* 2006, *Yemaya,* 2000)
www.yasminhernandez.com

Women Warriors of the Afro-Latina Diaspora / edited by Marta
    Moreno Vega, Marinieves Alba and Yvette Modestin.
        p.   cm.
    ISBN 978-1-55885-746-9 (alk. paper)
        1. Latin American literature—Women authors. 2. Latin Ameri-
    can literature—African influences. 3. Blacks—Latin America—
    Ethnic identity. 4. Women and literature—Latin America. I. Vega,
    Marta Moreno. II. Alba, Marinieves. III. Modestin, Yvette.
    PQ7081.5.W68 2012
    860.9'9287--dc23
                                                        2012008327
                                                        CIP

♾ The paper used in this publication meets the requirements of the
American National Standard for Information Sciences—Permanence
of Paper for Printed Library Materials, ANSI Z39.48-1984.

12 13 14 15 16 17 18   10 9 8 7 6 5 4 3 2 1

Table of Contents

PERSONAL CONTEMPORARY

Acknowledgements

Inter American Foundation

Ford Foundation

Dr. J. Michael Turner

Sandra Garcia

The Franklin H. Williams Caribbean Cultural
Center African Diaspora Institute

GALCI/Global Afro-Latino and Caribbean Initiative

Katherine Lutz

Michele Avery

Veena Mayani

Tony Van der Meer

Dara Cerv

Red de Mujeres afrolatinoamericanas,
afrocaribeñas y de la diáspora

Encuentro Diaspora Afro

All of the women and men who have
supported the birth of this project

To Sonia Pierre for her work with Haitian Dominicans and her sacrifice—her life.

To all the women who continue this journey.

Introduction

MARTA MORENO VEGA, MARINIEVES ALBA AND YVETTE MODESTIN

THE TRANSNATIONAL AND GLOBAL COMMUNITIES THAT THE movement of Afro-Latinas and their families are experiencing reflect the need for understanding, for redefining and restructuring definitions and practices that address present conditions. For example, Afro-Latina/o communities in Colombia are targets of paramilitary forces that are trying to displace them from lands that are rich in natural resources. Afro-Latinas in Brazil and the Dominican Republic continue to combat poverty while being promoted to the world as "sexual objects" within their countries and as cultural exotic tourism opportunities. At the same time, progress is being made. Epsy Campbell's success in forming part of a new political party in Costa Rica, through which she ran for vice president of the country, certainly indicates hard-won opportunities. But even with such examples of progress, the lives of African descendents are still primarily framed by a marginality that continues to foster poverty, as well as by the lack of educational, fair housing and economic opportunities. What is different is that there is a growing political activism headed by women of African descent. These women are creating an international movement that will have a positive effect on their families and communities.

Recognizing and celebrating the place of Afro-Latinas in contemporary global society also means accepting the social, economic and political dislocation of these communities, and honoring the freedom fighters, change-makers and everyday people who fuel the Afro-Latina/o struggle for holistic development. Contesting illusory notions of a multi-racial utopia in which European, indigenous and African descendents live harmoniously without addressing the effects of colonialism, imperialism and enslavement, *Afro-latinidad* not only demands recognition for the historical presence and contributions of African descendents since the end of the transatlantic slave trade, but also heralds a shift with regard to how Latin American identity is constructed today.

From North America to the Southern Cone, the concept of Afro-latinidad in the Americas continues to stir deep emotional responses while inspiring local, national and international movements for racial justice and equality. Challenging both Eurocentric constructions of Latin American identity and narrow U.S.-centered constructions of "black" identity in the Diaspora, Afro-Latinas/os are demanding their place in history as purveyors of resistance and as the progeny of a deep-rooted legacy. Afro-Latinas are indisputably at the heart and the helm of this struggle.

Who are the women who lead the struggle against inequality and social, economic and political underdevelopment? Who are the frontline warriors—organizers, cultural workers, teachers, politicians and healers—who are cultivating the next generation of the movement's leadership? Furthermore, who is the next generation? How does Afro-Latina identity shape the place of that generation in the world? How is that identity defined?

Women Warriors of the Afro-Latina Diaspora reflects the
voices of Afro-Latinas who are actively committed to visions
of equity and justice in all aspects of their lives and of their
communities. The writers are Afro-Latina activists who are
committed to transforming the historical legacy of racism and
discrimination that continues to hold Afro-Latinas and their
communities at the periphery of their nations' development.
The contributors span a range of professions from grass-root
community scholars to academicians, elected officials and
international policymakers. They are women who have faced
the barriers of race, education, class and gender to create
spaces of liberation from which to battle their governments,
international agencies, and sometimes the fears of their own
communities. Grounded among their people, they use their
positions to advocate for justice, racial equality, cultural equity and human and civil rights.

The life stories of the women featured in this anthology
are known within their countries and influence national and
international policies. Yet their lives and their work remain
virtually unknown outside their linguistic cultural contexts.
This anthology seeks to provide the general public with access
to the life stories of remarkable Afro-Latinas. The life stories
of these writers offer insight into the lives of more than 150
million African descendents who reside in Spanish-speaking
countries in the Caribbean, the United States and Latin
America.

Increasingly, migratory and immigration patterns indicate
that the population of Afro-Latinas/os is a large part of the
U.S. population descended from Africans. Cubans, Puerto
Ricans, Panamanians, Dominicans and other cultural groups
from Latin America and the Caribbean are changing the
meaning of the term African American within the United
States. This confluence of Afro-Latinas/os and other African
descendents and Africans from the continent has created an

international population of the African Diaspora within the United States. These cultural encounters have developed and deepened an informal interlocking dialogue among communities of African descent. This conversation was further solidified during the United Nation's World Conference Against Racism and Discrimination in 2001.

The role and activism of Afro-Latinas in making the issues of African descendent communities visible within their countries and to international communities are virtually unknown. In *Women Warriors of the Afro-Latina Diaspora*, these pioneering women share their empowering stories and encourage others to share theirs. Their stories provide insight into the conditions that have led Afro-Latinas to challenge systems of inequity, including the "machismo" that is still prominent in Spanish-speaking cultures. Most importantly, the anthology communicates that "ordinary" women are extraordinary when they commit to a dream and seek to transform adverse realities. Each of the women writers is deeply engaged within her community, working on the ground locally as well as in international settings to bring attention and solutions to the legacy wrought by more than four hundred years of African enslavement in the Americas. At the UN's Conference of 2001, which took place in Durban, South Africa, it was women such as Sergia Galván, Dorotea Wilson and Nirva Camacho who framed the strategic agenda for Afro-Latinas/os by lobbying for the visibility of more than 150 million African descendents in Spanish-speaking countries.

The story of these women's lives will resonate with readers who question their color, their purpose in life and their future. Each story is unique, yet each contains points of similarity with the others in that they all wrestle with the issues of human rights, social justice, race, gender and visibility, respect, intellectual property and power. The essayists and poets are women who have faced the barriers of race, education, class and gender to create spaces of liberation from which to battle their governments, international agencies, and sometimes the fears of their own communities. Many are grounded in their communities and use their positions to advocate for justice.

Wrestling with these issues requires extraordinary personal commitment and risk-taking. The women whose stories are contained in this anthology possess these qualities and have used them to leap above confining barriers in order to create a vision of racial and social justice. Their stories invite us to confront our barriers.

Historical

Afro-Venezuelan Cimarronas Desde Adentro

NIRVA ROSA CAMACHO PARRA

T O BE A DESCENDENT OF AFRICANS IN VENEZUELAN SOCIETY has many implications. Afro-descent implies an historical past associated with slavery—a culture identified mostly with music, dance and drums—and belonging to a lower-income social class, as if these attributes were inherent to this population. This evaluation becomes even more complex when one adds being a woman to the equation—gender inequality and gender-related prejudice come into play.

Many Venezuelans still are unaware of the great legacy of Afro-descendents, from which they have derived benefits unknowingly, and which should make Afro-descendents deserving of greater appreciation. In Venezuelan historical documents, the struggle of maroon women leaders and comrades alongside African men who fought their enslavement at the hands of the Spanish empire remains hidden in the few references that mention the resistance of African slaves.

We, Afro-Venezuelans, represent struggle, resistance, determination and intelligence. We have made great contributions to our country's economic, political, social, cultural and religious development. Yet, today we are forced to continue to be on the lookout for many different aspects of racial discrimination.

1

Knitting My Identity

Being born to an Afro-Venezuelan family—considered as one composed mostly of Venezuelans, with the phenotypic characteristics and/or cultural practices of African ancestry—established my childhood identity as part of a particular ethnic collective, although at that time I did not understand its dimensions. Being black was considered normal, perhaps because I lived in a community where everybody had similar physical characteristics. My dark skin and "bad" or "toasted" hair was not a problem.

I grew up in a family where my parents placed great value on getting an education. My mother wisely said, "Although I was unable to get an education, my daughters, I want you to study because that is all I can give you." She believed that our inheritance lay in the knowledge that we could obtain through academic studies, without realizing, perhaps, that many of the values and customs she taught us were part of the great legacy that would transform us into the women we eventually became.

I started becoming aware that because of my blackness others might consider me different when, as an adolescent, I began attending a school outside of my community. There I was exposed to classmates with different shades of skin (some white) and different types of hair (including straight). There I started being categorized as one of the darkest-skinned black girls in school, although many people's reactions did not yet feel discriminatory in nature.

Later, "despite being black," as racists might say, I was accepted into the School of Psychology at the Universidad Central de Venezuela (UCV, Central University of Venezuela), one of the most prestigious universities in the country. There I began to experience racial discrimination—I started to become aware of the racist feelings and beliefs of non-black persons. For example, one of my classmates once remarked, "How typical of blacks," and on seeing me exclaimed, "But of course, you're an exception!" This, and many similar experiences, contributed to my growing self-perception that I was part of a "privileged" few black women at the university, where despite being a public institution, manifested class divisions that affected the school's environment, placing many Afro-descendents at a disadvantage.

In this environment I began to learn that class structure often gets mixed with race; there is not only prejudice and discrimination against people of lower social classes, but also against people of color. What I could determine at the time was the origin of these racist ideas, since in the school little was taught about the history of Africans in Venezuela. There were no classes exploring the subject and, consequently, there was no knowledge of the great contributions of Africans to the political, social, economic and cultural development of the country.

Racial prejudice and discrimination continued to make itself known in different ways—sometimes openly and at other times subtly: however, I had finally become aware that my being black was a motive for differentiation and exclusion.

Getting Involved in the Afro-Venezuelan Movement

I received my degree in Psychology, and although I could recognize racism, I still could not see its transcendental nature and its multiple implications for individuals who were victims of it. One day, a co-worker invited me to participate in a group of women fighting against racial discrimination. Through this group I became aware of other possibilities; other horizons became visible. Being rejected because of my physical characteristics was no longer a personal perception—there were others like me in the same position. I needed to understand the workings of racism and find the means to fight it.

First Encounter/Re-Encounter

The group was the Unión de Mujeres Negras de Venezuela (Union of Black Women of Venezuela), an organization that many people considered segregationist, exclusionary and full of women with inferiority complexes. In this group, I met women of fortitude who spoke with firmness and certainty about the importance of women's rights, and of black women's rights in particular. These women caught my attention and marked a new phase in my life. I felt like I was re-encountering myself. They were black women like me, many of them professionals: Irene Ugueto, a social worker; Josefina Bringtown, the first black woman doctor in Venezuela; Reina Arratia, who had invited me to join the group and Marisol Guevara, both of whom were social workers; Yudith Rada, a biology professor; and other women in a variety of occupations. What was most important to me, however, was their self-awareness, their knowledge of who they were, where they came from and the why and how of their skin color and their physical characteristics. Through the group, these women were trying to tease out the ins and outs of the racism that exists in Venezuelan society, a society that considers itself non-racist and egalitarian.

It was the 1990s. I became a member of this organization, the only one of its kind in those days. From there I came into contact with many other women's organizations that had linkages to the union, primarily though the Coordinadora de Organizaciones no Gubernamentales de Mujeres (CONGM, Network of Non-Governmental Organizations for Women). The CONGM brought together, at the national level, many different groups with a great variety of interests, testifying to the rich diversity of Venezuelan women: feminists, indigenous women, black women, environmentalists, domestic workers and so forth.

In this group, my life's project began to take shape, a project different from the one I had imagined for myself, but not contradictory to it. Indeed, it was complementary, since I had chosen two people-related professions: nursing and psychology, the physical and the psychic. Now I was learning how these two aspects of human beings combine with spirit, history and culture. I was experiencing the essence of being. Recognizing who I was, learning how I identified myself with certain physical and behavioral characteristics that were based on certain values whose origin I didn't yet understand clearly, although I knew that I had learned them from my parents, and that they, in turn, had probably learned them from my grandparents.

In 1991–92 we implemented a project in a black community in La Sabana, Vargas State, the town where Irene Ugueto came from. She was the president of the group, the main spark, the untiring student of the issue of racism. The project involved the development of tourism in that community, starting with historical reconstruction using the methodology of research in action, so that the townspeople would participate in and own the process. They were able to identify part of the historical memory of their community, how it was founded, where their ancestors came from, why they were not owners of the lands on which they lived. The project did not crystallize in its second phase, which involved the conversion of part of their homes into B&Bs for tourists. This part of the project required debt financing, and many participants were afraid to assume the debt. The project did yield, however, the rediscovery of much of the community's history and collective memory.

Another important activity of the group was the public campaign to expose the existence of racial discrimination in mass media and nightclubs. We organized two national meetings of black women to debate the situation of racism and racial discrimination in its various manifestations.

From the Physical to the Spiritual

In 1993, approximately three hundred women from the countries of America, Africa and Europe gathered for the Sixth Conference of the Institute of Transcultural Women's Studies.

The purpose of the conference was to analyze the reality of women of African descent after five centuries of resistance to the European invasion of the American continent.

At the time of the conference, Irene was fighting not only for the rights of black women and men, but also for her own life, confronting her illness with great courage. Irene died in December; she departed in body, but she left us a great legacy of conscience and commitment to continue the struggle. She was a catalyst of the struggle for women's rights in Venezuela, particularly the rights of Afro-Venezuelan women, and her spirit continues to fight with us. She was an example and a symbol of determination in the fight for our rights, the search for our origins and the reaffirmation of our ancestral values. She was a pioneer in this battle in our country and left important footprints in the contemporary history of Afro-Venezuelans. She was an activist with firm convictions who could see clearly the destination for her Afro-descendent brothers and sisters. She founded the African-American Studies Center at UCV in the 1980s, and participated in many women's events at the national and international levels. She became a fundamental example for many of us, who were infected with her dreams and hopes for a more humane society for all.

In 1994, Josefina died as well. She was another pioneer in the movement who left us her own teachings. She was the first black female medical doctor in Venezuela, and she was spoken of as such in the media. The members and owners of the media betrayed, perhaps subconsciously, their own racist beliefs. To them it seemed incredible that a black woman could obtain such a title. As a doctor, she dedicated herself to the community where she was born, Barlovento, Miranda State, an area where many Afro-Venezuelans had settled, where there had existed and still exist, many cacao plantations. Josefina dedicated her life not only to her profession as a doctor, but also to social work. At the Union of Black Women, she took on many responsibilities to monitor and expose discrimination against women, in particular those of African descent. Like Irene, she participated in national and international events that addressed the reality of black women. She died with the conviction that she had contributed greatly to building hope for an egalitarian society.

How to Continue?

Despite these losses, we chose to continue our fight—to abandon the struggle is forbidden! How does one leave what has become a part of your life? How does one unlearn the value of the fight for equality and respect for human rights, specifically those of the Afro-Venezuelan population, whose rights were constantly trampled in a subtle manner? The leadership of the organization was passed on to Reina Arratia, another one of the founders. We felt the absence of Irene and Josefina, but learned little by little how to continue without their physical presence, accompanied instead by their spirits.

There were some changes: some members left and others joined, and the group continued participating in the CONGM, joining forces with other women's organizations. We provided capacity building to women in an Afro-Venezuelan community regarding women's rights, family violence and racial discrimination. We participated in national and international events. In 1996 we formed an alliance with the Afro-American Foundation, led by Jesús "Chucho" García, an organization with which we had something in common. That year we had joined in a study on race funded by the Inter-American Development Bank (IADB). This alliance marked the beginning of a new phase in the work to combat discrimination.

On a personal level, in 1997 I completed my graduate degree in family education and counseling, for which I wrote a thesis entitled "Values in the Afro-Venezuelan Family and the Role of the Consultant-Counselor." My awareness of issues related to Afro-descent had changed: I was now equipped to perceive the reach of discrimination. Not only was I a descendent of Africans or one of the few black women in graduate school, but also I had now learned to decipher how discriminatory messages affect the minds of black people, or rather Afro-Venezuelan people, as I want to name us from now on, and to keep in mind the many aspects of the individual.

The research of Sherzert and Stone: "When counselors do not know or understand members of the various subcultures to whom they provide counseling . . . they ignore important data that has much influence on behavior" (226).[1] This message confirmed for me the connection between the profession I had chosen and the struggle I was fighting—that I had to take into account when working with my patients, their culture, their ethnicity, their specificity.

As of 1999, the Union of Black Women and the Afro-American Foundation were participating in the Afro-America XXI, an international Afro-descendent movement, which had been established in response to the IADB study mentioned above, and we jointly organized an international conference on the family. In 2000, we called on other national organizations to form a network where we could combine forces and enhance the work we had been doing individually in our regions. Thus began the Red de Organizaciones Afrovenezolanas (ROA, Network of Afro-Venezuelan Organizations), of which I was a founding member.

The network has initiated many activities in which women have provided a leadership role. The main objectives of the women are:

---

[1]See Sherzert, B. and S. Stone (1980). *Manual para el asesoramiento psicológico*, Buenos Aires: Editorial Paidos.

- to increase the educational and informational level of women in Afro-Venezuelan communities, with the understanding that such an increase will foment the development of the family;

- to implement actions to promote the self-discovery of African descendents, with a biological and cultural specificity, but with equal rights to participate in society;

- to promote education and capacity building in productive areas that will contribute to improvement in the economic status of Afro-Venezuelans and their families;

- to monitor the realities and issues that specifically affect the lives of women, such as sexual and reproductive health and the discrimination in compensation, and how these issues are interlinked with ethnicity;

- to promote the participation of Afro-Venezuelan women in governmental and non-governmental activities affecting women, at the national and international levels, in order to ensure the incorporation of the ethnic-Afro-descendent perspective as a cross-cutting dimension in women's struggle.

With these objectives in mind, we began to develop the political agenda of Afro-Venezuelan women. So far, the ROA has organized four national conferences to debate our situation as descendents of Africans and plan how to promote the transformation of Venezuelan society. In 2004, at the third national conference, the women decided to establish the National "Cumbé" of Afro-Venezuelan Women as a space to deliberate issues that affect women differently from men, such as family violence, sexual and reproductive health, the labor market and racial discrimination when it is combined with gender issues. Bringing a gender perspective into the larger

group has been received in different ways: some men understand what we are talking about, others seem not to.

What is most important is that we women have advanced
much along a path that at first seemed much rougher, when in
1999 the Union of Black Women of Venezuela and the Afro-
American Foundation jointly presented proposals to the
Venezuelan Constituent Assembly for the official recognition
of the Afro-descendent population in the new Constitution.
The proposal was not adopted, although many members of the
Constituent Assembly were Afro-Venezuelan.

More recently, the Cumbé has been developing a political
agenda that promotes our issues in education, the economy
and public policy. We have initiated a dialog with the Instituto Nacional de la Mujer (National Institute of Women) and
the Banco de Desarrollo de la Mujer (Women's Development
Bank), since they are institutions that implement public policies addressed specifically toward women. With the former, we
have taken steps to incorporate the Afro-descendent variable
in the Plan de Igualdad para la Mujer (Plan on Equality for
Women), although there have been no concrete results yet.
With the latter institution, we have begun a pilot project to
offer micro-credit financing to Afro-Venezuelan women. The
project is meant to promote economic development based on
customs, values and modes of production of African ancestry.

My militancy in the Afro-Venezuelan movement has
taught me how racism and racial discrimination affect my people, and it has awakened in me the desire to study and search
for ways to confront the many complex feelings generated by
my experiences. I have learned about the effects of our lack of
self-acceptance and how to help my Afro-Venezuelan sisters
and brothers accept themselves and deal with the rejection
and mockery of others. This knowledge has encouraged me to
address how racism affects each person according to the
resources and level of strength he or she possesses. Addressing

the issue at the level of the individual is indispensable for each person to be able to understand when her or his rights are being trampled, and what steps to take to reaffirm them. To start, I, as an individual, should be aware of who I am, where I come from and what I want from my life's work. The awareness of each person's individuality will establish the guidelines for the agenda in the Afro-Venezuelans' struggle in the political, economic, social and cultural realms.

My thinking about these issues led me to realize the need to direct more resources toward education, based on the hypothesis that knowledge of our past, as well as of the current reality of our community, will facilitate the embrace or reaffirmation of our self-identity. This, in turn, will help halt the various forms of racial discrimination in our societies.

Why Study Internal Racism?

The historical experiences of our ancestors in the Americas and the Caribbean left their mark not only on the socioeconomic and political structure of our societies, but also on the internal thoughts and beliefs of millions of men and women. Even today, men and women continue to suffer the consequences of the racism and racial discrimination that originated in the times of slavery and was justified with absurd reasoning. One aspect that the ideologues of human commerce failed to take into account was the psychological implications of slavery for those who were enslaved. No one cared what the enslaved thought or felt, why they committed suicide, why they rebelled—the latter two being mechanisms of resistance against their subjugation.

Today in the Americas and the Caribbean, children, young people, men and women descended from these African slaves continue to suffer the consequences of racial discrimination—an important manifestation of which is internal racism. Internal racism develops in an individual, perhaps as a defense mechanism, to deal with the multitude of negative messages and acts directed at him or her, which are internalized and crystallized as a self-image that the individual refuses to identify with.

I have defined "internal racism" as an auto-discriminatory attitude in which the person undervalues the physical and cultural aspects that identify him, in this case, as an Afro-descendent. At the same time, he overvalues the characteristics that could be interpreted as European, thus giving the person a sense of false superiority. This process has been observed in a large proportion of Afro-Venezuelans in the communities where the Network of Afro-Venezuelan Organizations and the Cumbé of Afro-Venezuelan Women have worked. Internal racism is a subconscious attitude in the majority of the population studied so far.

Racist ideas have resulted in a great number of prejudices in Venezuelan society, which are transmitted through a number of institutions that have the ability to reproduce this type of message. Chiefly among them are the family; the mass media, especially television because of its wide reach; churches, which label religions of African origin as satanic; and the educational institutions, which omit and distort the role of Africans and their descendents in the socioeconomic and political development of Venezuelan society.

Treating and overcoming the effects of internal racism requires self-analysis of the individual. It also requires the transformation of the system that reproduces these negative messages and stereotypes. To address change at the individual level, I developed an educational tool that facilitates the unlearning of racist ideas and their replacement with alternative behaviors. The process requires that the individual first learn about and recognize the contributions that African ancestors made to the sociocultural, political and economic development of their current society; second, understand that she or he is a product of a socialization system that often distorts anything related to the Afro-descendent population; and third, accept him- or herself, including the historical-cultural elements deriving from African ancestry.

Currently, I am doing research on the incidence and reach of internal racism in this population group, as well as developing alternative methods to eradicate it. Among these are self-discovery workshops designed to develop the individual in a holistic manner, which includes not only exploring the problem at the individual level, but also its larger implications in the context of social dynamics.

My research on women and men in Afro-Venezuelan communities—particularly interviews with women who have not yet had the opportunity to overcome the racist messages they have internalized—reveals that lack of self-knowledge and self-esteem makes it more difficult to decipher the racist and discriminatory behaviors of others and the ways in which these behaviors affect the social, political and economic dynamics of society.

Political Relevance, Accomplishments and Challenges

After understanding the personal process and its interlinks with social dynamics, it became urgent to establish mechanisms to control the psychological effects of racism, racial discrimination and internal racism, and to design, implement and monitor public policies to address the needs of the Afro-Venezuelan community. Major priorities include:

- transforming the educational system to include the Afro-descendent perspective, highlighting the contributions of Afro-Venezuelans, rather than continuing to reproduce the distorted history that has, until now, been written by neo-colonizers intent on perpetuating the false belief in the superiority of one racial group over another;

- developing indicators and collecting official statistics to determine not only the proportion of the population belonging to this group, but also where they live and their living conditions, in order to facilitate the design of policies to address their specific needs;

- studying the health status and the incidence of major diseases in the Afro-Venezuelan population and improving their access to high-quality services that guarantee optimum health;

- promoting provisions in the Venezuelan Constitution, as well as an anti-discrimination law to guarantee the right to a life free of discrimination.

To address these issues, the Network of Afro-Venezuelan Organizations and the Cumbé of Afro-Venezuelan Women have worked to facilitate dialog with the state, with the understanding that both the state and civil society are responsible for overcoming social inequalities. Fortunately, there have been some advances that promise greater inclusion of citizens of African descent in the continuing process of building a new model of society in Venezuela.

The new Venezuelan Constitution is a good start, although it does not specifically bring visibility to the Afro-descendent population. Its preamble reads: "The people of Venezuela . . . with the supreme goal of reshaping the Republic to establish a society that is democratic, participatory and self-reliant, multi-ethnic and pluricultural, in a State of justice. . . ." In Article 21, it affirms that "all persons are equal before the law, and, consequently: . . . No discrimination based on race, sex, creed, or social standing shall be permitted. . . . The law shall guarantee legal and administrative conditions such as to make equality before the law real and effective; shall adopt affirmative measures for the benefit of any group that is discriminated against, marginalized, or vulnerable; shall protect in particular those

persons who, because of any of the aforementioned circumstances, are in a manifestly weak position; and shall punish
those who abuse or mistreat such persons."

This opening in the legal framework has been used somewhat effectively by civil society to demand public policies that
address the Afro-descendent population. Today, there are some
spaces in governmental institutions that do just that. For
example, there is now a liaison office for Afro-descendent communities in the Ministry of Culture, a technical consultancy in
the National Institute for Women and a space in the Institute
for Youth. In 2005, the National Assembly declared May 10
Afro-Venezuelan Day in honor of José Leonardo Chirino, who
led one of the most important rebellions against the Spanish
Empire.

A presidential decree entitled "Prevention and Elimination of Racial Discrimination and Other Distinctions in the
Venezuelan Educational System" was issued. A presidential
commission was established to execute the decree. Article 1 of
the decree states: "The Presidential Commission for the Prevention and Elimination of All Forms of Racial Discrimination and Other Distinctions in the Venezuelan Educational
System has been created as a permanent entity. Its purpose
shall be to elaborate, formulate, coordinate, monitor and eval-
uate programs, methods and public policies concerning the
education sector, which shall guarantee equality of opportunities and treatment for all persons with respect to the enjoy-
ment and exercise of their right to education."

My participation in the Network of Afro-Venezuelan
Organizations afforded me the opportunity to be part of this
presidential commission, which currently promotes studies of
the Venezuelan educational system, including the structure
and services of educational institutions and monitoring of the
process of redesign of the educational curriculum. It also stud-

ies the different discriminatory practices of teachers, students, parents and guardians.

The decree also provides for the design and implementation of anti-discrimination measures in communications. The commission is preparing a proposal for a communications policy based on respect for diversity and equality of conditions for the various population groups. The commission takes into account cultural aspects as a cross-cutting consideration in all of the activities it pursues.

Dancing with Hope

The dream of an egalitarian society, with equality, justice and freedom from discrimination, remains in the minds and spirits of all of us who sow conscience and knowledge of our identity, who seek our origins, our past. We act to transform the present and build a better future, where diversity is understood fully, differences are respected and equality is cultivated.

The challenge facing the Afro-descendent social movements in Venezuela, particularly the ROA and the Cumbé of Afro-venezuelan Women, is a continuing commitment to promoting changes that will free society of racial discrimination, where each person can learn to know him- or herself with respect to ethnic characteristics and fight to improve his or her quality of life, and where the Venezuelan state continues to advance in recognizing its co-responsibility to formulate public policies that address the Afro-Venezuelan reality. As activists, our challenge is to continue knitting strategies to combat racial discrimination and internal racism, even when faced with a lack of comprehension of our rights on the part of the various sectors of Venezuelan society, which often includes the very Afro-descendent population that is the victim of internal racism. Our challenge is to clear the way for future generations to enjoy a fuller life.

Carrera de una cimarrona

MÓNICA CARILLO

¡Corre,
      fuga,
           salta,
                araña!

llegaste al monte
nadaste el río
el verde del
Pájaro Bobo
te envuelve
aquí no hay selva
como en Palmares
tampoco los ríos
de Esmeraldas
aquí la pampa
te pega el polvo
en las narices ...

¿Adónde iré si hay cordillera
o un horizonte que me descubre?

Confío y rezo
orado el cerro
invento un oasis
pero no vuelvo
primero asalto
asusto o mato
como mis heces
y me alimento,

el perro ladra
huele mis pasos
ya no retengo
ni mis respiros
todo lo dejo
en el camino
para que cuando
me muerda el anca
no reconozca
mi cuerpo esclavo

porque si muero
entre sus dientes
moriré libre
no "liberada"
por alguna gracia

él ya escapó
y no volvió
quizá me espera
y sueña verme,

(tal vez la pierna
que llevó el perro
hacia la hacienda
no era de él)

quizá el destino
nos acompañe
el perro ladra,
aquí no hay selva,
el monte es bajo
llegué hasta un río
que va hacia el mar . . .
¿por qué me llevas
sin esperanzas?
¿ya no hay consuelo
en esta vida?
veo al cielo
atormentado
por mi partida.

(Orula Orula
OruOrulaOrula
no seas severo
dale caricias Orula
no seas severo Orula)

hay un barranco
y me deslizo
amaso el barro
mientras gateo
no hay más silencio
escucho cantos . . .
vuelve esperanza

veo fuego . . .
es un palenque
que me recibe
allí esta él,
hay un vacío
en sus rodillas

                    (la pierna se la
                    llevó el perro)

pero él me espera
siempre de pie
como los árboles
como un guerrero
bajo una máscara
hecha de troncos

ya no estoy sola,
ya no estoy sola,
tengo a mi axé
tengo a mi axé
tengo a mi axé.

Personal

Bodies and Memories: Afro-Latina Identities in Motion

ANA-MAURINE LARA

T HE SPACES THAT AFRO-LATINAS IN THE UNITED STATES
occupy are undefined spaces that result from the ways in
which race has been constructed in U.S. society. Because
of these constructions, and the institutions built around them,
many Afro-Latinas are often not seen by Black Americans or by
other Latinos. We must, in turn, push to be seen. The tenden-
cy among those of us who occupy this space is to go to the fear
that "Afro-Latinas" and "Afro-Latinidad" lack definition. The
response to this fear is often a desire to generate an essential
articulation of identity and place: the notion that Afro-Latinas
are one thing, or come from one set of places/experiences/
histories.

In this essay,[1] written in the personal voice, using personal pronouns, I will critically analyze the construction of Afro-
Latina identities in the age of globalization. I will be using my
body and identity, as well as the creative works of various
Afro-Latinas as examples for my analysis, which includes:
defining Afro-Latina bodies, flushing out Latina identities in

---

[1] Parts of this essay are based on another essay entitled "A Change of
Manta" published in *Telling Tongues: A Latin@ Anthology on Language
Experience* (Calaca P/RedSalmon P), 2007.

the United States and making connections between the placement and the liberation of Afro-Latina bodies.

The Language in Which I Speak

In order to discuss Afro-Latinidad, I think it is important
to first understand that race and racism are constructed differently in different societies, though their application may be
the same (the control of colored female bodies by bodies that
are not colored or female). Because we live in the age of globalization, and at a time where U.S. commodities, including
cultural productions, are being propagated throughout the
world en masse, I think it is important to lay the groundwork
for my analysis on U.S. terms. There is, however, a caveat
because these commodities include the sale and distribution of
Afro-descendent bodies (in all forms of art and cultural production), whose distribution re-enforces already existent
notions of race and belonging that reify U.S. myths around
white supremacy. Simultaneously, because we are discussing
Afro-Latinas, I am bringing in concepts that have shaped my
particular experience as an Afro-Dominicana. These concepts
have their own history, separate from the history of the United States, though still grounded in the policies of colonization
I think they are very much affected and re-enforced by U.S.
racial constructs disseminated by globalized media.

I live in the United States, where the myth of racial purity is based on two other myths: whiteness and the one-drop
rule. I was born in the Dominican Republic, in the Caribbean,
where the myth of racial purity is based on three other myths:
hispanidad, blanqueamiento, indianismo (Hispanism, Whitening, indigenous). For the purposes of this essay, I will define
these terms with an understanding that I speak as someone
who is based at the heart of the empire:

Race is the social and economic value ascribed to a person
or group of people based on perceived shared phenotypical

characteristics (pigmentation, eye shape, facial form, etc). I believe this is a concept largely developed in the wake of colonization, specifically to justify the economic practice of the exploitation of some bodies by others.[2]

The concept of *racial purity* grew out of the race-based eugenics movement of the mid-nineteenth century. This scientific movement based on evolution and improvement of human heredity suggested such methods as selective breeding, birth control, genetic engineering and genocide of those deemed inferior. The foundation of the myth of racial purity is that there are separate races of humans, which should not mix so as to preserve the purity of blood lines.[3]

The term *whiteness* is used to refer to the socioeconomic and political privileges and powers ascribed to people who are phenotypically European or Caucasian. Because it is a concept that has been ascribed power and meaning, it has concrete violent ramifications on the lives of people who do not participate in whiteness, directly or indirectly.[4]

---

[2] In the beginning phases of Spanish colonization, there emerged several rationales for enslaving the indigenous populations. Bartolomé de las Casas, among other Catholic clergy in power at the time, wrote to the Spanish crown about the grave abuses in the treatment of indigenous peoples. The logic of the Spanish colonial leadership led to the importation of *ladinos*, ie., Christianized Africans already working as slaves in Europe, and finally of *bozales*, ie., un-Christianized Africans, which Nicolás de Ovando stated, "los nacidos en Africa se mostraban más sumisos y resistentes a las duras faenas de las minas y la elaboración del azúcar" / "the Africans born in Africa seem more submissive and resistant to the harsh conditions of the mines and sugar cane plantations" (Deive 54). This is one of the first examples of the logic leading up to racist policies, whereby the phenotypical characteristics of a people identified by geography are used to qualify and justify their enslavement.

[3] U.S. concepts of racial purity are preceded by documents, such as the Carolina Black Codes of 1685, the edict of King Luis of France y Navarra, enacted in the Iberian colonies.

[4] For a radical, organizing definition of whiteness, refer to the Challenging White Supremacy workshop paper: "What is White Privilege?" http://cwsworkshop.org/resources/WhitePrivilege.html.

The *one-drop rule* is specific to the United States and was
first used unofficially in the nineteenth century to determine
the status of slaves, and then later on officially established as
law in the early twentieth century at the onset of the Jim
Crow era. The main purpose of the one-drop rule was to
enforce racial purity and whiteness.[5]

Hispanidad refers to societies that were once under Spanish
or Portuguese colonial rule, and as such, are constructed on
the moral and ethical values of Iberian humanism, Catholicism, the Spanish and Portuguese languages, Iberian last names
and blood. It is the notion that these societies are unified under
these values, without conflict or question. It has been applied
in nationalist rhetoric to evoke the supremacy of the state over
individual communities and bodies—specifically, bodies that
evoke non-Iberian references (Indigenous, African and Asian
bodies in the colonial context).[6]

Blanqueamiento literally means whitening. It is a social concept based on and upholding *hispanidad* as the ultimate goal of

[5] For further discussion about the one-drop rule, see *Who is Black? One
Nation's Definition* (Penn State UP, 1999), by F. James Davis. An excerpt
from this work is available online: http://www.pbs.org/wgbh/pages/front-
line/shows/jefferson/mixed/onedrop.html. Many other authors cite the
one-drop rule discussion, including Naomi Zack, Neil Gotanda, Michael
L. Blakey, Julie C. Lythcott-Haims, Christine Hickman, David A.
Hollinger, Thomas E. Skidmore, G. Reginald Daniel, Joe R. Feagin, Ian
F. Haney-López, Barbara Fields, Dinesh D'Souza, Joel Williamson, Mary
C. Waters, Debra J. Dickerson among others.

[6] In the Dominican Republic, Trujillo used the concept of *hispanidad* to justify the ethnic cleansing of Haitians and to consolidate the power of the
oligarchy. For further discussion of *hispanidad* in the Dominican Republic,
refer to Joaquín Balaguer's *La Isla al Revés*. In the Dominican Republic,
hispanidad was a discourse that led to the development of policies on presentation (dress codes), identity (races on national I.D. cards) and religious practice among many others (the outlawing of *voudou*). One of the
goals of this discourse was limiting "the spread of Negro influence across
the West Indies" following Dominican independence from Haiti in 1844
(Torres-Saillant 127).

individuals and families in society, placing great value on the attainment of presumed European phenotypic characteristics (blue/green eyes, straight hair, light skin, etc) in offspring.[7]

Indigenismo is used primarily to refer to literature, but also refers to the social construct of the "noble Indian," an indigenous person with a romanticized past. As such, *indigenismo* has been evoked in Dominican nationalist discourses as a way to erase African history and presence by replacing it with Indigenous, Taíno[8] or Spanish identity.

I will be employing these very basic definitions and these two specific sociopolitical contexts (the United States and the Dominican Republic) as the setting and frameworks for my analysis.

Defining Afro-Latina Bodies

Florinda Bryant, a self-defined Black-Mexicana, created a hip-hop theatre piece titled "Half-Breed Southern Fried Check One" that critically engages her lived experience as the

---

[7] "*Blanqueamiento* refers to the processes of becoming increasingly acceptable to those classified and self-identified as 'white.' This is an ethnic movement—coterminous with socioeconomic advancement governed by the ideology of 'development'—that depends upon socioeconomic and political assistance and loans from the developed (i.e., highly industrialized, highly energy-dependent) countries. Although not often recognized as such, the ideology of 'whitening' is an unconscious psychological process accompanying the economic state of underdevelopment in the twentieth century. *Blanqueamiento* essentially accepts the implicit hegemonic rhetoric of the United States with regard to 'white supremacy' and often blames those people classed as black and indigenous for the worsening state of the nation" (Torres and Whitten, 1998, pp. 8-9).

[8] I think it is critical to note that there is a Dominican Taíno movement; exerting Afro-Dominican identity does not and should not cancel out Indigenous struggles for liberation. Unfortunately, these have been played off against each other in Dominican discourse on culture and identity. What I am referring to is the blatant omission of African descent in the discourse, replaced by a call to Indigenous identity—a political strategy which served to disenfranchise both people of African and Indigenous descent.

daughter of a Mexican/Tejana[9] woman and a Black American man. In this piece, she discusses not only the complexity of her lived experience, but the reality of race relations in the South and particularly in Texas.

Written in a hip-hop aesthetic, the protagonist in the piece recalls a memory from childhood, when on the first day of fifth grade, the teacher, Ms. Butler, goes through roll call, and in the process asks for the children's race.

Ms. Butler: Florinda Bryant? Florinda?
Student 5: Here.
Ms. Butler: Race?
Student 5: Mixed, Black and Mexican.
Ms. Butler: What?
Student 5: I am mixed. My momma is Mexican and my daddy is Black.
Ms. Butler: I see, well we have to report your race. Let's just put African American.[10]

This excerpt to me not only highlights the conflicts arising out of "outlaw" unions, such as the marriage of Blacks and Mexicans/Blacks and whites/Blacks and Asians, etc., but also the particular dilemmas faced by Latinas who are of African heritage. On the surface, it is difficult to tell the difference between what the protagonist's body signifies and what could be defined as her lived experience: her body is a Black Latina body that is simply read as a Black female body in the South. On a deeper level, beyond the surface, what we find is a complex weave of social constructs based on race and nationality.

---

[9] The implicit assumption, within the U.S. social landscape, is that with the national/ethnic Mexican identifier, the subject/object is not of African descent.

[10]"Half-Breed Southern Fried Check One," performed at UT-Austin on September 8, 2006 as part of the Center for African & African American Studies "Performing Blackness" series.

In sitting with the piece, I couldn't help but wonder how the conversation would be different had the protagonist been born of two Mexican parents, one who was Afro-Mexican and the other who was not. Of course, that would overlook the specific complexity of the protagonist's story: because of where her body is (Texas), and because of what her body is: a symbol of the union between a Black American, sharecropping, cowboy history and a Mexicana church-going/border crossing/ Spanish-speaking herstory.

Later on in the piece, the protagonist enters a moment of self-reflection, almost as if provoked by the constant assumptions thrown onto her physical body:

Whose legs do you have? Whose hands do you have? Whose eyes are those?

I walk like my dad/whose legs do you have? Hold cigarettes just like my daddy/whose hands do you have? eyes like my Aunt Alice/whose eyes do you have? hair like my mom/whose hair do you have? What do you see in the mirror/all over your body. I sound like my sister/whose voice do we have? I sleep like my grandmother/drink like my grandfather/what do you see? When you look at your body. Wide hips/high cheek bones/Not sure who we don't remember. What do you see written on your body. All this blood with so little truly our own. I walk like my dad, hold a cigarette like my dad with my mom's hair.

What do you see? What does your body remember?

Florinda Bryant, as the writer, takes the protagonist from a space of contemplating the physical embodiment of heritage to the ephemeral recollection of ancestral memory, ending with "What does your body remember?" while simultaneously touching upon the notion of blood. "All this blood with so lit-

tle truly our own." With these two statements, Bryant highlights the rift between expectations and lived experience.
What are Afro-Latina bodies supposed to experience? What
do we really live? Whose children are we? What do our bodies
demonstrate to the world, and what does it remember? Simultaneously, Bryant asks us to consider notions of African and
Indigenous ancestral memories and the "one-drop rule" of
blood and racial purity.

As Afro-Latinas in the world, we are constantly negotiating others' assumptions about where our bodies and our memories overlap, where our Blackness/*negritud* begins and our
Latina-ness end. As Afro-Latinas in the United States, we are
also negotiating the notion of blood and racial purity in a way
that was obscured in most countries under Iberian colonization. In the Latin American context, rather than quantifying
race by one drop, Iberian laws connoted gradations of racial
categorization based on specific mixtures of blood. This simultaneously obscured *negritud* and made blackness central to
Criollo identity all at once, in that the official number of
"*negros*" decreased, while the number of "*mestizos, pardos,
mulatos, zambos,*" etc. increased. In the United States, with
the one-drop rule, whiteness became central to racial identity
formation, and polarized people into essential categories. It is
this tension between centrality and essentialism that plays out
when an Afro-Latina body walks through spaces in the United States.

This space of tension, of lack of clarity, of shifting and re-
definition is at once the most painful and one of the most liberating and complex areas of lived experience.

Taking Florinda Bryant's writing as a cue, and using my
own body as the location of analysis, I have laid out some of
my responses to some of the questions the protagonist in "Half
Breed Southern Fried Check One" asks as a segue into looking
at these shadowed areas. These responses serve to complicate

the dialogue and demonstrate, *en carne viva* (in the flesh), the ways in which Afro-Latina identities and bodies transgress essential categorization.

Whose eyes do you have?

I don't know what my father's mother looked like, only that she made love with "*un moreno*" and my father was born a dark, mahogany brown. The implication in the floating whispers is that she herself was not *morena*, or dark in any way, that she transgressed. She died when my father was young. He was raised by his grandparents and everyone calls him Negrito. This term of endearment both obscures his darkness and brings it to light.

When I was eighteen and visiting my family in Santo Domingo, as I had every year since we left, I said to my light-skinned, light-haired cousin, "My father's *negro*, that's why everyone calls him Negrito." My cousin said, "No, he's not. He's *moreno*. They call him Negrito because they love him." I had to insist, "Yes, that's true. But, he is *negro*. And that's not a bad thing." My cousin shrugged his shoulder and shook his head. He thought I was crazy, insisted I was insulting my father. I thought he was crazy for missing the obvious.

I think I have my father's mother's eyes. Nobody else has them. Nobody else is willing to see the beauty of our darkness.

Whose hands do you have?

A Trinidadian friend of mine puts lotion on her hands and kisses each finger after she is done. She insists that it's important that "our hands not look ashy" and that "You've got to love your hands." When I was younger, white people would tell me, "You have such healing hands." I would nod, wondering if they were transferring racist implications on dark skin, or if, in truth, I was born to heal. I look down at my brown hands and wonder whose they are. At first glance, they look

like no one else's in my family. They are a rich oak brown, full
of lines on big, big palms. They're callused, no matter how
much lotion I put on. I have small fingers, short fingers with
curves on the end of them. At second glance, I realize they are
my mother's hands. Mine are brown, hers are white. I don't
know, though, where the healing powers came from: the ability to take away pain by touch or to soothe fear by holding.

Whose hair do you have?

When I was growing up, my Dominican cousins Yadira and
Rosanna would spend hours "combing" my hair. Rosanna, vio-
let brown and with a head of tight, kinky hair, would try to pull
out as much as she could and Yadira, yellow (my *tía* says she's
jabao) and with *pelo grueso*, ie., nappy hair, would try to put
back as much as she could. I would be at their mercy until my
Tía D. showed up, smacking their hands with the combs and
leading me into her bedroom to repair the damage. She would
sit on the bed and have me stand between her legs, with a tube
of Vitapointe on her thigh. She'd rub my scalp, fill her palm
with the hair grease and pass it through my hair. "*Niña*", she'd
say, "*tú tiene el pelo bueno. No deje que esas niñas te lo dañen.*"
(Little girl, you have good hair. Don't let those girls damage it.)
I didn't understand what she meant by *pelo bueno*. When I
wasn't with her, I was in another country, with white European
and American kids who made fun of the way my hair puffed up
when it was dry, or the way the curls set against my head. My
well-intentioned, but ill-informed, mother was taking me to
white hair dressers who would giggle nervously and say, "Isn't
that sweet? She doesn't even need a perm," as I sat under their
scissors. My father would come to my room at night and tell
me, "Make sure you brush your hair a hundred times every
night. That's what Abuela does." He, with the kinks wound
tightly against his head, was proud of my "good hair."

Whose legs do you have?

My legs are the thick legs of women who grew up farming or working in the mountains. They are not necessarily feminine, and because they're what I walk on, I understand that they make me seem masculine. I'm okay with that. To me, it's part of my legacy to be a masculine woman. I come from a line of women who worked outside, and the work inside—it was necessary in order to survive. Because of class—and I mean rural poor—my female ancestors were always seen as masculine, because they weren't middle class and they didn't hold to middle-class aesthetics of femininity, because of race.

I know that for me, embodying both female and male energy is necessary if I'm going to pull ahead. How else could I do my healing work: the work of healing bodies, memory and land? I am not a *partera*, whose feminine energy is what allows for the path between the womb and this life to be continuous. I work with my hands and my vision in a different way. I write stories, I garden, I tend to medicine plants, and I use my hands to transfer the pain into the earth. All the while, my legs hold me. My legs are strong. They're hairy. They're dark. I know that if I had to, these legs would carry me to the deepest recesses of the mountains where no one could find me. I know that these legs have done that before.

What does your body remember?

I am an Afro-Dominicana, not only because my skin, eyes, hair, lips and hips say so, and therefore, indicate what everyone else will perceive. I am an Afro-Dominicana because in the context of white supremacy and in the history of my transnational experiences, I know that to walk in the world as an Afro-Dominicana is to honor my African legacy and the struggle of my ancestors in working the land. My cells know this to be true. I know that the soil is a deep mahogany red because of my ancestors' blood. Here, on this mainland, at the heart of empire, my body remembers the taste/feel/smell/sight of soil from the land where I was born, and everything that happened from the moment of my first breath until now. My body is the place where people's expectations, fears, desires and assumptions are constantly negotiated. My body remembers its journey and its ancestors.

Walking with Ancestors

I didn't always know about my ancestors. They were hidden in layers of family secrets, or stored away in my aunt's basement waiting for the dust to be blown off of their captured images. Some of them have no graves to speak of, and others are set in beds of stone, concrete and steel. What I do know is that part of my family was forced to this hemisphere under the conditions of slavery, and that the other part of my family bought people and forced them to work as slaves.

I first learned about my ancestors through my name, Ana-Maurine Higginbotham Lara. It is an ancestral name, of sorts. Ana, I was told, was given to me because it is easy to pronounce; Maurine is my maternal grandmother's name; Higginbotham, the name of my maternal grandfather, is the name that connects me to the legacy of slaveowners and freed blacks in the United States; and Lara is the name of my paternal great-grandfather, a farmer, a mulatto, a descendent of faceless Spanish men and unnamed, faceless black women.

I then learned about my ancestors through storytelling —over the dinner table, at family gatherings, through the laughter of familial jokes and memories, through the tears raised by death. I learned that Aunt Mattie was a painter and that Don Enrique won the lottery. I learned that after we had been here for several hundred years, working the land that belonged to others, my family squatted on some land that they called their own.

I wrap myself in my ancestor's stories. I look at their photographs, I search for compassion in myself to forgive them for whatever harm they may have done. I listen for their guidance. They have made it possible for me to be here today, and in recognition of this, I use their lives as lessons.

My ancestors are necessary to my work as a healer. Because my role is to heal those who come to me, regardless of where they have been, social constructs have no relevance. In dealing with peoples' bodies, spirits and emotional and intellectual vulnerabilities, I have to exercise the highest discipline to do the healing work. Because my ancestor's stories are complex, and because their stories are realized in my flesh—my lips, my eyes, my skin, my laugh, my ears, my walk, my illnesses and my gifts—I am often called to understand that my present body is an amalgam of theirs. The only answer I have for sure is in their stories.

Afro-Latina Identities—The Story of Califas[11]

It took me leaving the Atlantic Coast to understand the profound importance and significance of the Middle Passage in my life. When I moved to California in 2000, I lost my Latina identity: that is, the people I thought were my people, didn't see me as their people. It was the first time in my life I had been stripped of something that I thought was so thoroughly and collectively inherent. The Califas Latinos/Xicanos/Mexicanos took one look at my black skin, my *mulatta* features, my curly hair, they listened to me speak, a funny kinda speak . . .

---

[11]Califas is the Chicana/Xicana term for the current state of California. It is a play on language originated by pachucos in the early twentieth century, as well as a reference to California having been a part of Aztlán. My choice to use the word "Califas" to designate California is a signifier of the ways in which my own Latina identity(ies) have been shaped by Chicana/Xicana consciousness. For more on the use of the word Califas, refer to "Calafia/Califas: A Brief History of Chicana California" by Amalia Mesa-Bains or Manuel Cantú's *Pachuco Dictionary*.

like that of somewhere else, and figured I was an African-American woman who had learned to speak Spanish.

I mean, I know there are people of African descent in Mexico!! Even if Univision doesn't "find" them, portray them, etc. (unless of course we are maids in a Venezuelan *telenovela*). However, everybody and their *abuelas* watches *Sábado Gigante*,[12] and even if Don Francisco insists on hiring the whitest,[13] skinniest women he can find to dance and entertain, he would be nowhere without the colored audiences. One would think that with the large number of Puerto Ricans and Cubans in Califas, that perhaps invisibility wouldn't happen so much, but I was very shocked to find that it did. Again, and again, and again. Even though everyone and their mothers was dancing *salsa* and *merengue*, and drinking *mojitos*, I was invisible. I was no longer Latina in other peoples' eyes, which ended up having real consequences.

I went to a Latino caucus at a U.S. national conference of organizers held in the Bay Area. A black Panamanian friend and I were almost barred from entering. Here is the transcript:

---

[12]*Sábado Gigante*, a show that is broadcast on local stations from the tip of Chile to the cold riverbanks of Montreal, is the most far-reaching and longest running TV program in the Western hemisphere. Just by virtue of visiting family, I am often subjected to it. Every time I go to my sister's house on a Saturday, it's on. Nobody's watching, but it's on anyway.

[13]Contrary to popular dialogue about race in Latin America, I do purport that there is a class of white people in Latin America who are invested in their whiteness. It is not whiteness as we understand it to be in the United States, but one that is based on notions of "purity" of Spanish/European blood that is deeply tied into the history of the ruling colonial master class. As U.S. television reaches deeper into peoples' homes, this notion of "hispanidad" is also being conflated with U.S. notions of beauty based in Anglo-Saxon ideals of whiteness. In other words, the more "Spanish" you are, and the more you "look American"/"act American" while still not being American, the higher social status you are accorded.

Woman at the Door: You are in the wrong place, this is
  the Latino caucus.
Me and Friend: Yes, we're Latino.
Woman: But, the caucus is in Spanish.
Me: I speak Spanish. (My friend stood silent, he doesn't
  speak Spanish.)
Woman (visibly annoyed): Well, come in.

We walked in among the stares and whispers and sat down
on the floor. Two Mexican *jornaleros* (day laborers), were talking about working as farm laborers and the issues raised by lack
of documentation, changes in California laws and such. I
knew about their struggle because I could see everyday how
jornaleros stood in desperate lines on César Chávez Boulevard,
waiting for a pickup truck to take them somewhere to work,
often vulnerable to police or INS harassment. I had worked to
overturn some of the California anti-immigrant propositions,[14] and had seen those efforts fail.
  As they spoke, I couldn't help but think about the connections between the *jornalero* struggle and the struggle of
female garment workers on the East Coast, a struggle that was
very close to home. I raised my hand: "What about the NYC
garment workers?" The women in the room stayed silent. The
conversation continued without addressing the connection. I
raised my hand again, "I understand what we're talking about,
and I think we need to connect it to the struggles of the gar-

---

[14]Specifically Proposition 209, the California Civil Rights Initiative, dismantled state-level affirmative action when it passed in November 1996
affecting thousands of people of color. This was passed after Proposition
187 (1994; overturned 1995) had already limited immigrants' rights to
health and education, and right before Proposition 227 (1998), which
eliminated bilingual education. The language and spin of each of these
propositions ended up pitting Black Americans against Latina/os.
MALDEF and other civic and political leadership organizations led
strong state-wide organizing initiatives to educate Latino voters, who in
the end, voted overwhelmingly against Proposition 209.

ment workers on the East Coast." At this point, everyone was annoyed. I was told I was out of place. "For what," I asked. "*¿Ser mujer, negra, caribeña o joven?*" The caucus leaders, men, stopped looking in my direction. I was given the stares. People whispered to each other. It was so painful. Here I was thinking it was a "national" gathering, only to find out that national Latino agendas meant that some issues, experiences, language, sex, gender, struggles, ways of being in the world superceded others, and that radical women, people of color, were participating in these patterns.

Yes, I was naïve. But rightfully so. I was from the East Coast. I had been organizing in Boston for six years, where Latina/o DID encompass everything from the farm workers, to the *jornaleros*, to the garment workers, to the families that had arrived by boat, plane, foot, train, etc., to the women, the men, the queers and the professors, where Latina meant Dominicana, Salvadoreña, Mexicana, Xicana, Boricua, etc. I was naïve and shocked. I realized, in that moment, that I was going to have to figure out how to connect with people in Califas on completely different terms. I understand that in that space I am an Afro-Latina first and foremost, and could therefore be systematically excluded from Latina/o conversations and initiatives because of racism.

Years before, back in the mid-1990s, when I was twenty years old and was in San Francisco for a summer internship, I got into a huge argument with my friend, Tia. Tia was African American, from the islands off the coast of Texas. All her life, she had grown up around Black people and had never interacted with people who weren't Black until she left the island at the age of twenty-four to go to San Francisco. Even then, she made family with other Black folks. We had become friends through work, and often hung out together in the afternoons playing pool or drinking a beer. That afternoon, I was winning (at least I'd like to think I was) our game. I can't recall how we started our conversation about race, but pretty soon, the game was over and we were into it, the IT being a discussion about Latino-ness and Black-ness.

Tia: I don't understand Latinos.

Me: What do you mean?

Tia: I don't understand why Latinos insist on wanting to be white.

Me: I don't think that's true.

Tia: Well, take you for example. How do you identify?

Me: I'm mixed, but as a Latina, I'm of African descent.

Tia: So you're Black.

Me: No, I'm not Black. I'm of African descent.

Tia: But you're BLACK!

Me: I'm Latina of African descent.

Tia: But you are *Black*.

Me: I'm not! I'm of African descent, but my blackness is not about being from the United States.

Tia: But you're BLACK. I'm Black, you're Black. She's Black, she's Black. Black! (Tia pointed out the window at two sistahs walking by. I shrugged my shoulders.)

Me: I'm not denying that I'm of African descent, but I'm not Black. My history of blackness is not a U.S. American history. On my American side, my mother's white, a descendent of slave owners. And I'm a Latina of African descent—my peoples lived through slavery in the Dominican Republic, not the U.S. It's different.

Tia: I don't care what you say. You still Black.

Me: Well, fine, if that makes you feel better. But don't get mad at me when I start speaking to you in *español* and dancing *salsa*, or if I'm asking for *morro* and not rice and peas.

This entire interaction was not only a spat about internalized racism, it was also an evocation of very real, very palpable
tensions between people born in the United States and those
born outside the United States who are of African descent. I
know now that as a twenty-year-old, I was relying on my experience of race up until that point in time, and what I thought
I knew was that "Black," as an identity, belonged to people of
African descent born in the United States, and that that identity evoked specific cultural values, norms and points of view
that were different from the ones I was familiar with. If we had
discussed whether or not I was *negra*, there would not have
been a discussion. I would have said, yes, I'm *negra*. If we could
agree that to be of African descent included divergent experiences, then yes, I could be Black. Tia could not know that I
was sitting in the midst of tensions between Black Americans,
black English-speaking Caribbeans, Haitians, Dominicans and
Puerto Ricans. Every Black American I had come into contact
with, until that day with Tia, had insisted I was not Black; or,
just as intensely, embraced me as Black American until they
realized that I was from the Dominican Republic. So for me,
my response was in recognition of my lived experience—that
to call myself Black American was false, because my connection to the Middle Passage is through the Spanish-speaking
Caribbean.

All that changed when I actually moved, five years later, to
Califas to live. After I realized that many of the Latinas and
Latinos around me were not trying to even create connections
between genocidal histories, in all honesty, I had to stop and
question my Latina identity. I ended up landing in the space of
Afro-Latinidad on a whole new level: spaces of Africanity and
U.S. Blackness became my home away from home. Even
though the experiences and ancestral memories were different
for myself and people from the United States, there was an
unspoken understanding that in the white supremacist world

we were all moving as black bodies. This commitment to my identity took on an additional level of meaning when I moved to the Dominican Republic in 2003.

Afro-Latina Identities—Moving Across Borders—the Story of Santo Domingo

In 2003, I moved to Santo Domingo, Dominican Republic, to live. I thought I was going to be there for the rest of my life. I was never going to live in the United States again. I ended up there for only nine months, mostly because I couldn't get a job. That piece had everything to do with my perceived race and class. At the time, I had dreadlocks. They were thick and swung around my head like snakes. They held a ton of power, and I could feel my crown and my third eye pulsing under their weight. They were spectacular for healing work. As a woman, they set me apart from other women. In Santo Domingo, they set me apart from everyone. I couldn't go into businesses or banks without setting off suspicions; no one would hire me because of my "appearance"; I was constantly harassed by the police.[15]

The most ironic moment came to me in an entirely unexpected way. I was taking a class at a private institution. By default, most of my peers were young, upper and middle class. Because I was older, but also because of my appearance, no one spoke to me. I knew my experience was not unique. A close friend of mine, who is slightly older than me and darker than me, also had that same problem in the classes she was taking. So, taking her experiences into account, I went about my day without paying the students much mind.

One day, during break, I sat down in the courtyard. This young dark-skinned woman sat down next to me and struck up

---

[15]The police are always harassing people; however, they were harassing me because they thought I was a black man.

a conversation. She directly asked me about my locks. After I explained to her that I had locked my hair for spiritual reasons, and in solidarity with Black people around the world, I watched her eyebrows go up as she exclaimed, "But you're not *negra!*" I looked at her carefully, noting that she was darker than me, with straightened hair that was streaked with blonde highlights. I shook my head, thinking about whether to intercept with some consciousness-raising, or to listen to what she was thinking. I listened. She said to me, "Look, we're descendents of Spaniards and Africans, *por cierto*. There's very little Indian. So we're mostly Spanish and African." I nodded. She continued, "But, I'm racist. Against Haitians, that is."

This statement, unfortunately, did not surprise me. Having studied Dominican concepts of race and ethnicity, I had come to understand that in hegemonic discourses "blackness" in the Dominican context is equated with Haitian-ness, and that Haitian-ness is equated with numerous assumptions about the social value and worth of dark-skinned people. These assumptions are embedded in the social, political and economic structures of the nation, and limit the livelihoods of dark-skinned people across the country. The discourse of *anti-haitianismo*, as it is known, originated at the end of the nineteenth century, and became deeply conflated with notions of Dominican identity, across several generations, in the twentieth century. Race became embedded in national identity, thus making it possible for an admission of African ancestry and of racism against those who represent the reason for that African ancestry.

I asked her, "Why?"

She said, "Well, I wasn't alive for those twenty-two years of occupation,[16] but I am angry that they occupied this country. I think they are trying to take over the island. They are

---

[16]The island of St Domingue/Santo Domingo was unified under Dessalines' rule between 1822 and 1844.

trying to take over our country. And I don't like the way they walk."[17]

At this point, I decided to do an intervention. I pointed out gently that Haiti lacks the resources for a takeover, and that Haitian franchises and billboards weren't the ones popping up all over the country; that is unless Pizza Hut, Pepsi, Coca Cola, Wendy's, McDonalds, Burger King, Baskin Robbins, Haagen Dazs, Hilton, Verizon, Hollywood Cinemas, Outback Grill and all the "free trade zones" are Haitian and I just didn't know. She nodded her head, trying to understand what I had suggested. I promptly excused myself and left.

This entire scenario was only possible because I reeked of U.S. American privileges, both in the way I looked and in the way I walked. It doesn't matter that I was born in the Dominican Republic and that I claim connection to the land. The fact that my body had transgressed national boundaries and settled for some time on U.S. soil meant that I was inherently different—something about me was changed. What was changed was my deep consciousness of race. Not only had I learned about U.S. racism while in the United States, I had learned about Dominican forms of racism as well, and this was only possible because I was an Afro-Latina body that was shifted by global market forces: my family moved to where the jobs were. As a result, I had lived in the United States and became politicized and acculturated here. So, it was ironic that I, dreadlocks and all U.S. privilege, was sitting with someone who had to straighten her hair in order to get employment, in a place where I was being ignored because of my presentation.

---

[17]I'm often struck between the similarity in discourses around Latina/o immigration in the United States and Haitian immigration in the Dominican Republic. Both discourses use nationalism to perpetrate racist ideologies of humanity and nationalist ideologies of race, but in vastly different ways.

I could afford to be indignant because I could leave to get a job elsewhere.

Defining Liberation from One Afro-Latina Context

I believe it is a political imperative to tell our stories and to construct as varied a definition of our existence as possible, in as many ways as possible. Only then can we be free in the world.

Years ago I set about writing a novel, *Erzulie's Skirt*. I wanted to write *Erzulie's Skirt* not only because the characters were pestering me day and night, but also because I knew that it would unlock an internal dialogue in Latina/o and U.S. African-American communities around, defining liberation on Afro-Caribeña terms: What does freedom and liberation mean for me as an Afro-Dominicana, but also what kinds of terms could I define, in a creative body, for the liberation of Afro-Caribeñas in general?

I knew that in order to entertain that dialogue, the context of the story would be incredibly important: Where are Afro-Latina bodies found? For me, we are found everywhere, but most importantly, we are still mostly found in places of labor, especially in the Dominican Republic, where "appearance" and class go hand in hand.[18] Secondly, because of globalized political and economic forces, our bodies are also found

---

[18]"Ser negra es no tener 'buena presencia'; por tanto, será difícil para nosotras encontrar espacios de trabajo que sean valorados socialmente. Nunca les pasará por la mente la presencia de una negra en trenza, o el pelo sin desrizar, al frente de una empresa, de un banco, recepcionista, secretaria o en mostradores de líneas aéreas, por ejemplo. Por nuestras condiciones fenotípicas, sencillamente no somos aptas para estos puestos." (Curiel, 1996, p.117) [Being black is not having "good presence"; therefore, it will be difficult for us to find employment that is socially acceptable. People never imagine a black woman with braids, or with hair that has not been relaxed, as a CEO of a company or a bank, as a receptionist, secretary or as a customer service representative for an airline, for example. Because our phenotype simply disqualifies us from such positions.]

in transition from place to place—between islands, between homes, between the past and the present, between dreams and the waking world. We leave the *conucos* (small family farms) and go to the garment factories—either in the city of our homeland or across the water in the United States—in search of a better life for ourselves and our children. We also go to New York, Massachusetts, Texas and California. We also go to college. We also go back "home".

I also decided that in order for me to explore the world view of the characters, I had to understand their histories, ancestries and dreams. *Erzulie's Skirt* is clearly a work of the African Diaspora. It dares to create an African baseline in the story, thereby creating a direct link between Dominican Africanity and the slave trade, a link that has long been obscured by discourses on Haitian-ness as Blackness. I wanted to uncover the *cimarrón* history in my country of birth, to uncover the spaces of Black pride and strength, to give them validity within a fictional world in order to create room for an analysis in the non-fictional lived reality of the everyday. I wanted to allow the characters to be unflinching in their truths.

I am definitely not the first Dominican American novelist to embed the characters in an Afro-Dominican worldview. Nelly Rosario does so in *Song of the Water Saints*,[19] Loida Maritza Pérez does so in *Geographies of Home*.[20] I am also not the first writer to utilize her lived experience to explore the power of language to shape our worldview. Florinda Bryant did so in "Half Breed Southern Fried Check One." Together, our works span an unessential definition of Afro-Dominicanness, specifically as experienced in female bodies.

In *Geographies of Home*, a young woman is changed by her departure from her home in Brooklyn, inasmuch as her family has been changed by their departure from the island. In *Song*

---

[19]New York: Pantheon Books, 2002.
[20]New York: Penguin Books, 2000.

of the Water Saints, daughters and mothers struggle with their personal freedoms as the world around them shifts and as they shift in and out of it, transitioning from one context to the next. In "Half Breed Southern Fried Check One," the very fact of language and memory changes what the protagonist believes to be true.

What is important to me, in understanding these works together, is that they demonstrate that Afro-Latina bodies are not constricted to a particular experience or truth, and the characters that develop in our creative productions dare to live their lives despite essential expectations. No matter where our bodies land, we can generate fluid spaces that affirm our existence and our collective memories.

Works Cited

Bryant, Florinda. "Half Breed Southern Fried Check One," performed September 8, 2006 as part of the Performing Blackness Series at the University of Texas–Austin.

Curiel, Ochy (1996). "El prejuicio racial desde los derechos humanos y en una perspectiva de género". In *Memoria del foro por una Sociedad Libre de Prejuicio Racial*. Santo Domingo: Casa por la Identidad de las Mujeres Afro.

Deive, C.E. (1996). *Vodú y magia en Santo Domingo*. Santo Domingo: Editora Taller.

Mendoza, Louis G., and Toni Nelson Herrera (2007). *Telling Tongues: A Latin@ Anthology on Language Experience*. Aztlán: Calaca P & RedSalmon P.

Sábado Gigante (2007, January 13). In *Wikipedia, The Free Encyclopedia*. Retrieved 20:07, February 16, 2007, from http://en.wikipedia.org/w/index.php?title=S%C3%A1bado_Gigante&oldid=100402533.

Tolentino-Dipp, Hugo (1992). *Raza e historia en Santo Domingo: Los orígenes del prejuicio racial en América*. Santo Domingo: Fundación Cultural Dominicana.

Torres, Arlene and Norman E. Whitten, Jr. (1998). "An Interpretative Essay on Racism, Domination, Resistance, and Liberation". In *Blackness in Latin America and the Caribbean*, ed. by Arlene Torres and Norman E. Whitten, Jr. Bloomington, Indiana: Indiana UP: pp. 3-33.

Torres-Saillant, S. (1998). "The Tribulations of Blackness: Stages in Dominican Racial Identity." In *Latin American Perspectives*. 25(3): 126-146.

Memories of a Black Woman Activist

Diva Moreira

AUTOBIOGRAPHIES ARE NOT COMMON AMONG BLACK women activists in Brazil. It seems that we are embarrassed to speak about ourselves. I had always thought the appropriate thing was to die first so that someone else could write my biography. But when I received an invitation to contribute to an anthology of black women activists from the diverse corners of this, our suffering America, I was so excited, because I could review these decades of activism and also share with English speakers my experience and dreams. In this anthology of essays, we are telling our own histories and recovering the mosaic of our memories.

Whenever I reflect upon my life, I usually say that three things sustained me: my mother, a good public school and my faith in Jesus Christ.

Everything began with my mother, Maria de Jesus Moreira, a black woman who was the daughter of a black man from the coast (as my grandfather called himself) and a woman who was a descendent of the Tapuia Indians (as my grandmother used to say). My mother was a woman of exceptional courage and virtues. She was a domestic worker on a farm estate and got married very young. Shortly after my oldest sister, Inês, was born (in 1937), my mother became a widow. My brother, Paulo Afonso, was born in 1944. His father was a white man who was my mother's boss on another farm where she worked. I was born in 1946, and my father was a white man whom my mother met while working as a domestic worker at a boarding house. The sexual use of young black women by white men was very common all throughout the Americas. My mother's role as a domestic worker meant that, in addition to her domestic duties, she would have to fulfill sexual ones as well with very little room for negotiation, given the dynamic of unequal power relations between white male bosses and poor black women subordinates.

We moved to Belo Horizonte in 1950. My mother dreamed of giving us a better life than the one she was lead-ing. She sent my oldest sister to live with her parents, and my brother stayed with a couple she knew. She did this because she knew she would not get a job as a live-in domestic worker with three children.

Being an illegitimate child really marked me. In addition, I lived with many other stigmas during my childhood. While I know that stigmas are not unusual, they seem to be especial-ly common for black women in the Diaspora. Just think about it: I was the daughter of a widow, I was fatherless, I was black and I was a domestic worker. I began helping my mother in the boarding house when I was seven/eight years old. Back then, teaching a child how to work did not carry the same negative connotations it does today. It wasn't an exception. It was the norm, especially for black children. Today such work would be called child labor.

I experienced racism and humiliation at a very young age. The worst experiences were when my mother's bosses did not want me to continue attending school after the fourth grade because "blacks don't need to study more than that." They would turn off the lamps as I was doing my homework in order to hinder my academic progress, but I would light candles and finish my homework anyway.

It was horrible being a teenager who lived in other peoples' homes, suffering restrictions, humiliations, and sexual abuse (luckily, very mild thanks to my mother's protection). It was like living in two worlds at war: the white, middle-class educated one and the small black world of my illiterate and poor mother.

Beginning in 1959, I had the positive experience of attending the state-run junior high school, the Colégio Estadual de Minas Gerais. Anyone who studied there was proud to be there because of the school's quality teachers and prestige. I was one of very few black students in that elite public school, which was housed in a beautiful building designed by Oscar Niemeyer, the world-renowned architect. Even with all the rigorous lessons, heated debates about nationalists and sellouts invaded our classrooms. This was during João Goulart's presidency, and many reforms were being discussed and some began to happen. This was a period of enriching political education, where rules and authorities were questioned by the most engaged students.

It was also significant that the acting governor, Magalhães Pinto, placed his daughters in the school. Decades later, I established one criterion for the quality of public services for government use.

In 1963, we finally moved from our boarding house after thirteen years in Belo Horizonte. My brother decided to leave his step-parents in the north of the state to live with us, because he dreamed of joining my mother again. We went to live in a small shack in a neighborhood called Bairro da Serra and later moved to a small apartment (this was very fancy, compared to where we had lived: a double room "house") in a tenement. Even though I was embarrassed to be living in the "little *favela*" (slum) and used to hide it from my friends, it was

in that tenement that some of the most important moments of
my life occurred. I became involved with the youth movement
of the Catholic Church at the Dominican Convent. At that
time, the military dictatorship had not begun, and we lived in
an atmosphere of great debates and involvement in social
movements. The first time I heard the name Karl Marx was in
the convent. It was then that I began an intense relationship
with the Catholic Church, which provided me with great
friendships with the priests and nuns who instilled in me a
profound commitment to religious values on a personal level,
and to social movements on a collective level.

In 1968, I left my activist work within the church and
became a member of the Brazilian Communist Party. I was
excited by the ideas and political dedication of José Francisco
Neres, who in the 1980s would father my daughter Ana
Tereza. Although the Communists tried to convert me to
atheism, I continued being a Christian who was moved by the
idea that the egalitarian and just society that the Communists
spoke of was the earthly version of Christ's kingdom.

I explained all of my choices to my mother, who not only
agreed with their necessity but actually contributed to the
movements. She marched in the rallies against the military
dictatorship, cooked for the clandestine meetings of the Communist Party and participated in the feminist and prayer
groups of the church. She never feared the consequences of
my political involvement, nor did she ever ask me to be cau-
tious. She felt very proud to say that she participated in the
movements not just because of me and José but rather because
she believed they were necessary to combat all the injustice
she saw around her.

I was a member of the Communist Party for twenty years;
it proved to be another valuable space of political learning.
During that time, I was involved with various struggles of my
generation, including the fight against the military dictator-

ship, a regime which lasted twenty-one years. Most of my efforts were through the union movements and the Catholic Youth Workers because my brother was a member of that group; they were never through the student movement, which I felt was too elitist.

In 1970, when my mother and I moved into our home (one of the greatest moments of her life and mine), I began participating in community movements to improve urban conditions. I have the honor of fighting for sanitary reforms and for the creation of the Unified Health System. I also became involved in the reform of psychiatric hospitals in Minas Gerais.

The military dictatorship's attacks against the Communist Party in Minas Gerais in 1976, and the subsequent imprisonment of many of its leaders, including my partner, José, made it difficult for us to continue operating clandestinely. We all had to migrate over to the Brazilian Democratic Movement. This party ended up uniting many of the forces that were fighting against the dictatorship because of the courage and integrity of its members.

The suffering of the families of the victims of the military dictatorship led us to create the Feminist Amnesty Movement in order to pursue amnesty, to support political prisoners with monthly visits to prison and legal assistance, and to give their families our social support and solidarity. The idea of gathering women, mostly prisoners' relatives, was designed to transmit a kind of innocent image to the political police.

As a result of my various activities, my home was invaded twice—first by the CCC, which was a special group created to persecute Communists, and later by the Federal Police. In addition, I was called to testify at a hearing against the Communist Party, and I was being followed at the university, at the College of Philosophy and Human Sciences, because many of its students were involved in the armed struggle against the dictatorship. Furthermore, my name was on the list of enemies of the military regime, and I was forbidden to speak in public. It is important to say that I passed the entrance examination at the Federal University of Minas Gerais in 1967, which was a space for students from privileged families.

Many of us later became involved in the feminist movement, having been motivated by the assassination of a rich woman in Belo Horizonte. The woman was killed by her ex-boyfriend, and his defense was that he killed her to defend his honor. That absurd argument was frequently used in other cases involving famous women. The feminist movement's response was "Those who love don't kill."

The surprising thing is that I never became involved in the struggle for racial justice. Race never came up in any of the movements that I was a part of. No one ever asked me, "Diva, what does it mean to be a black woman?" "Have you ever suffered racism?" "Why is the situation of black people so different from that of white people?" Nothing was ever asked, and I never said anything. There was a heavy curtain of silence over the issue of race. Of course, I knew I had been discriminated against, but I didn't have a political consciousness of a problem that I thought only happened on an individual basis.

The first time the issue came up for me was while I was studying to get a master's degree in Political Science. I was the first black woman in the program. Professor Benício Vero Schmidt, a white, blue-eyed man, addressed me as a black woman and awakened my interest in the works of a Afro-Puerto Rican scholar by the name of Frank Bonilla. It was as if he had uncovered a cauldron filled with the silent desire to address issues of race. It was a relief! I was finally recognized as a black woman within an academic context, which was very important to me. That's when I began reading and attending events that dealt with racial matters, but, I did not become involved in the black movement until 1987. I was forty-one years old and had done nothing for my people. I had dedicated my time and energy to many democratic and liberation struggles, but I had never done anything for relieving the suffering of my own people. One day I was reading a book by Florestan Fernandes entitled *The Integration of Blacks in a Class-Based Society*. This book became a reference point for me, even though I would come to critique it later. The book discussed the obstacles that black people faced after abolition, including the lack of well-prepared leaders. Here I was, full of opportunities and so far removed from the black social movements. That book was the push I needed to join the anti-racist struggle. I did not identify with the MNU (Black Unified Movement), so I decided to create another organization, which was called Casa Dandara. The organization attracted countless people of all backgrounds, classes, education and political consciousness.

Once again, my mother was there participating in meetings and making meals for the study days, a race and political consciousness activity of our group. She was always encouraging me, even when I decided to leave a great job at the João Pinheiro Foundation in order to dedicate myself fully to Casa Dandara. We experienced very difficult financial moments after my pension finished. We lacked money to pay for everything: food, bills, transportation and so forth. At this point, my family was bigger because my daughter Ana Tereza had been born.

During this period, I was discovered by Cindy Lessa, the head of Ashoka–Innovators for the Public, a global non-profit organization based in the United States (Virginia) that searches and invests in social entrepreneurs who have innovative ideas and projects to change the life of their communities. I was selected for a three-year scholarship that allowed me to concentrate completely on the construction of an organization that would promote the rights of black people and would benefit the most marginalized segments of this population. To this day, Ashoka is still an invaluable space for learning and experience-sharing for me. I also received a fellowship from the Carlos Chagas Foundation, which financed reproductive rights projects with monies from the MacArthur Foundation. During this time, I worked with Adalberto Batista Sobrinho and Rubens Alves da Silva on a research paper entitled "The Triumph of the Whitening Ideology: Black Men and the Rejection of Black Women." This paper was widely accepted among black women, who commonly felt the sting of seeing black men reject black women. Actually, I still have the commitment pending to turn that paper into a book. I also worked as a monitor at the Interamerican Foundation. Unfortunately, not everyone at the foundation was excited about my insistence on getting the Foundation to fund anti-racist projects, so I was let go. Lastly, during this same period, the MacArthur Foundation funded another research project by me entitled "Racism in the Health Care Sector: Citizenship and Survival at Risk."

I always loved reading, and because there was such a scarcity of Brazilian works written about racial matters, especially by blacks conducting research, this became one of my most satisfying endeavors. I thought that black academics could write from a position of privilege because they wrote from the perspective of lived oppression by being part of the people who were thought incapable of constructing their own discourse. In this manner, black academics became subjects of their stories, as opposed to objects and could avoid many of the erroneous conclusions that other scholars arrived at.[1] The

---

[1] The books of economic history of Brazil are good examples of opposite and racist views on the causes of poverty and inequality. Important scholars accuse blacks and our culture of being the main reason for exclusion of blacks from the labor market after the abolition of enslavement. I can name Roberto Simonsen, Caio Prado Júnior and Celso Furtado, outstanding Brazilian economists, who adopted this interpretation.

other reason I liked conducting research was because I could remain up to date in current theories.

I think it is dangerous to become completely absorbed by activism because you lose sight of broader perspectives and become physically drained—something that African American women have termed "burnout." The competition among nongovernmental organizations also contributes to this burnout.

There seems to be certain cannibalism among us activists in which we tear each other down. It seems that words like love, compassion, solidarity and trust are foreign in our circles. This is wonderful for those who hold the power in our country. They know we don't love each other and thus are weak in our struggle against racism. For example, I don't call my experiences of conflict with other people in the black movement as political differences because I never really knew what the differences of opinion were between me and those who chose to demoralize and denigrate (Sisters: this is a racist term! This verb comes from Latin and means to become black, in a very negative way!) me and the work of Casa Dandara. I prefer the terms inter- and intrapersonal (What is that? I didn't like these terms either) and organizational differences.

We created a different way of doing racial justice work at Casa Dandara. We worked to create black identity and self-esteem, along with developing a critical consciousness about racial and political issues. We did all of this in a happy environment with cultural presentations during lunch breaks at our famous "study days." Well-respected professors from Brazilian universities would come in and lecture at our "study days."[2] The debates we sponsored during election periods were another important aspect of our work. Electoral candidates

---

[2] Jaime Pinsk and Ronaldo Vainfas made presentations during these "study days" in addition to Joãozinho Trinta, Marcos Terena, Ailton Krenak and other professors and personalities from Belo Horizonte.

were brought in to explain their platforms and also to be tested on their awareness of issues of concern to the black population. Members of our organization and visitors would come
in sporting buttons supporting parties from the right and the
left without ever feeling censored. Our space functioned as a
political education space accessible to people of varied educational backgrounds.

My next step in the struggle for racial justice was the creation of the Municipal Secretariate for Black Community
Affairs (SMACON) in Belo Horizonte. The municipal law
that created SMACON was approved in 1998 amid much
controversy. Many people argued that blacks were discriminated against because they were poor, not black, and thus
their needs could be met by social service programs. Some
even suggested that by highlighting issues of racism, racism
would be exacerbated. In other words, racism exists but we
should do nothing to address it because, by placing a spotlight
on the issue, matters could become worse. Others alleged that
SMACON would generate reverse racism because black people would be made aware of the discriminatory way in which
they were treated, would become angry and would in turn dis-
criminate against white people. To contradict these argu-
ments, I came up with an arsenal of responses. Among them
was that the state had a pressing responsibility to work to end
racism because racism was one of the main causes in creating
the miserable and substandard conditions in which the majority of black people have lived up to the present.

There was no consensus about my nomination for director
of SMACON. The black movement, like many others, is
divided into different factions without clear conceptual or
programmatic lines. Idiosyncrasies, power struggles and personal animosity are commonly masked as political differences.
It took a long and draining meeting for my supporters to convince my opponents that the mayor should choose me to

direct the organization, even without the creation of an administrative structure. Another important commitment was the guarantee that the community would be involved in constructing the programs and platform of SMACON, so as to avoid the frustrations faced by activists in other states where officials were involved in racial matters.

The impetus for SMACON came about after the mayoral inauguration in 1997, when the priority became building a support base in the Municipal Council so that the bill calling for the construction of the secretariate could be passed. This required me to pay the councilmen and councilwomen visits to educate them as to why this secretariate was necessary.

The media also provided a great deal of coverage. I was interviewed countless times in order to accurately represent and explain the goal of what would become SMACON. The mobilization of grass-roots support was so large that it created a favorable climate, and even all of the council members showed up on the day the bill was voted on. The bill was passed with a full house to much excitement. It was a historic day. This was the context in which SMACON was born; a year and a half later the mayor announced the proposal.

We were always clear that public policies alone could not solve the problem of racism. The idea was that SMACON would direct a movement that would begin a process to change the institutionally racist structures within city hall. We knew that our efforts would be worthless if there were no cooperation from the other departments of government. How could we achieve our goals when racism was denied, and never acknowledging the need for our specialized secretariate to address it? How would we overcome the stiff competition for financial resources?

It was evident that our next step was to build the legitimacy of SMACON within Mayor Célio de Castro's government. The mayor gave us the task of organizing a professional

school in one of the city's most dangerous *favelas*. Subsequent-
ly, all energies were directed to turning that school into a
model of efficiency and elegance, values important to what we
called "the black way" of governing. This decision generated
more outrage because it was said that SMACON was now
"invading the social services field." Despite the criticism and
lack of support, the school was extremely successful and often
lauded as an exceptional program at city hall.

It was extremely important that SMACON function as a
service provider while at the same time being seen as a solid
political project empowering black people in Belo Horizonte;
therefore, everything had to be done with great integrity and
aesthetics. By integrity, we meant that public policies should
create a sense of reciprocal responsibilities, of rights and
duties, from the government toward the people and vice versa.
The aesthetic dimension meant that people needed beauty
and elegance. Vandalism was a serious problem for city hall.
We defended the idea that people would not deface public
spaces if they were cared for in a manner that demonstrated
respect for the people they served. The professional school
that SMACON administrated had a beautiful garden, clean
and scented bathrooms and nicely decorated walls, which
were never vandalized while we were there.

Another important aspect of consolidating the secretariate
was our work with the poor. Throughout its existence, SMA-
CON worked in *favelas* and low-income neighborhoods. It
implemented one of the secretariate's objectives, which was
the institutional strengthening of the black population. We
prioritized this work specifically because of the social and
familial devastation faced by our people. These were the pillars
of what I termed "the black way" of governing. I was the first
black person to work as the director of a municipal secretariate
in the history of Belo Horizonte. As such, I seized the opportunity to introduce new practices, politics and programs.

Unfortunately, SMACON did not achieve all of its goals. Among the major reasons for this were the lack of support from the mayoral staff and the serious internal conflicts within SMACON itself. Employees who were against me, and even some of the ones I trusted, would boycott our work. The heads of division were members of the Workers' Party and had come to work in the municipal secretariate only for the purpose of creating an alliance that could oppose external attacks from some groups of the black movement. Unfortunately, such an alliance did not materialize because many of these same people "who were on our side" were co-opted by the members mentioned above.

I believe that the self-hate demonstrated within black social movements has not been adequately studied. The offensive attitudes and lack of respect, for me, by those Workers' Party members overtly contrasted with the leniency given to the white people who, in an abusive and authoritarian manner, destroyed four years of work dedicated to the most destitute segments of Belo Horizonte's population.

I left Belo Horizonte's city hall after SMACON was dismantled in a broad administrative reform imposed from above. I could not work for a government that behaved in a dishonest manner toward the black population. I did not lower myself to beg the mayor to extend SMACON's lifeline by promising I would be more understanding of and cooperative with the internal political hierarchy. I did not invite prestigious and influential staff officials to go to bars in order to gain their support or change their opinion that there was no reason for the creation of SMACON. The mayor had suggested that this was a good way to develop political support. To the contrary, I harshly criticized the mayor's decisions in the media.

I was unemployed for five months and experienced another moment of great financial hardship. My mother's unconditional support was now joined by my seventeen-year-old daughter's. My mother always used to say, "Those who bend over, show their behind." In other words, she was telling me that I could always make compromises, but never at the expense of my Christian and socialist ideals. If I needed to completely separate myself from something in order to continue holding my head high, then so be it. My mother didn't know the word consistency, but she used to tell me that she always prayed that my brother and I would never change, in the sense of letting good opportunities and prominent positions in life make us arrogant.[3] Our friends helped us a lot after I left SMACON. They lent us money and helped us with food. Even with our financial hardships, my mother and daughter never regretted supporting me in my decisions.

It is worth discussing here the fragility of the black family. Any disturbance among us leads to a major change in our lifestyles, and it seems that it is not as easy for us to regain status as it is for white professionals of the same level or even inferior levels. For black professionals, regardless of their national or international reputation, there is no safety net to prevent us from falling into unemployment and debt when we get fired. I believe that the fragility of our families explains the difficulty in achieving upward mobility and construction of a black middle class in Brazil.

My next position was as an assistant to the president of the Human Rights Commission of the Legislative Assembly. I did not work there for long. In August 2001, I left Brazil with my daughter, Ana Tereza, to participate as a visiting scholar at the University of Texas at Austin. It was there that I continued my studies and research on racial matters. Aside from being a wonderful academic experience, it was an extremely impor-

---

[3] Unfortunately my sister was not included in this regard, because she did not study at all. She got married at the age of seventeen, had eight children and ended up saying that, "This kind of knowledge does not enter my head anymore." Thus she cannot even sign her name.

tant time of reflection and healing. I had always been a full-time activist who allocated very little time to friends, family and myself. Being away allowed me the space and time to reflect upon my painful experience at SMACON. After Texas, I went to Washington to participate in a program sponsored by the Woodrow Wilson International Center.

I returned to Brazil in January 2003, and found the whole country in a state of euphoria because of Lula da Silva's presidential victory. I had read one of his interviews the previous year in which he promised to continue using the same policies as Fernando Henrique's neoliberal government; therefore, I was not enthusiastic about his victory, nor did I expect much.

I was unemployed until May 2003, when I was hired as a race and gender consultant by the United Nations Development Program (UNDP) in Brasilia. I think I was the second black woman to work in the agency. As always, I took my work very seriously. I am very thankful for the professional opportunities I have had in life. As a poor, black woman, I was a pioneer in many places where no black woman had worked before.

In September 2005, I was invited by the UNDP to be part of its office in Salvador, capital city of Bahia, in Brazil. I was told that I had been invited because the team needed an experienced and respected professional in order to guarantee the agency's success. I worked hard on fundraising and other activities, but six months later I was fired, allegedly for not doing my job. I was shocked because I never thought that something so lamentable would occur to me after fifty years of professional life, a life that I began as a child worker. I left after my dismissal, but I did contest what I felt was a defamation of my character and moral harassment at work. Unfortunately, I never received any response from the UNDP director. In addition to that painful dismissal in 2006, my mother passed away to join our ancestors. She was ninety years old. I grieved deeply because she was a wonderful presence throughout my life. Moreover, I felt guilty and blamed myself for being unmindful and obsessed so much with work that I had not arranged sufficient health care and assistance in her old age.

I don't want to end this essay with the sad story of my dismissal from the UNDP. From my time as a young activist in the Catholic Church, I learned to guide myself with constant hope, even though I must confess my disillusionment at various moments with the fragile democracy of our country. Brazilian society is very conservative and has not allowed social change and upward mobility for blacks. During the forty-five years of my involvement in social and political movements, I have not witnessed any structural changes affecting the social and economic conditions of the black population—certainly nothing comparable to the changes that have occurred in the United States since the times of the historic civil rights movement.

I believe that we, as racial justice activists, are also partly responsible for this situation. During the last two decades, the Brazilian state has been consolidating racial policy initiatives into ministries and government programs. In the past, many of us believed that this strategy would transform the lives of our people, and we began forgetting to build the foundations for change, particularly among those of us who are the most marginalized. Another problem has been the type of agendas we maintained, based upon specific social policies (for example, health care, curriculum reform, among others), but lacking connection to macro-economic policies. It is as if we thought it would be possible to resolve problems in one area without changing the Brazilian economic paradigm based on exportation and high payments of internal and external debt. In addition, those separate agendas made us overlook the dramatic matters that plague our people, such as poverty and violence.

We will always be at the mercy of white people, if the power structure isn't democratized, starting with political representation and participation in decision-making, and access to the media.[4] The opposite of wealth and power concentration is active citizen participation, and the lack of these public liberties is an obstacle to human development, as Amartya Sen states.[5] In other words, we are talking about the right of citizens to actively participate in the creation of culture, politics and economics, as well as monitoring human rights, without which we cannot close the immense gaps that divide our country.

Furthermore, our agendas based on specific topics and the need to get funding from the government, or from foreign agencies, made us overlook the need to work on the grassroots community level in the *favelas* and poor neighborhoods, in the prisons and in the landless and homeless movements. It is not possible to build social power when you are distant from the base. In my opinion, the best path to building power is through the slow and steady work at the base.

Lastly, in this globalized neoliberal world, we need to broaden our analysis and our action programs in order to address the reality of Afro-Latina women. I believe it is necessary to study the impact of neoliberal politics on the black population in the Americas. For example, the privatization of public services threatens our right to such basic necessities as water, sanitation and transportation.

The insufficient investment in social programs has destroyed the quality of the health care and educational systems, without which people do not have access to the job market. At the top of the list of problems that affect our community is the drug trade, which our young people are increasingly involved in. The conservative response has been to pass

---

[4] There are very few black representatives in our congress. In the State Legislative Assembly, despite the size of the black population in this particular state, there are few black representatives in office.

[5] See Amartya, Sen. (1999), *Development as Freedom* (New York, Anchor Books).

tougher laws and institute tougher punishment, as if they alone could resolve the problem of public safety, without addressing the deep-rooted inequalities and injustice in our society.

The problems facing our community are many. There is no doubt that we can confront them if we build inclusive and courageous political agendas and action programs. Even the smallest victories help us achieve higher heights in our struggle for the rights of our people. We also need to strengthen our national and regional networks. There are positive signals on the horizon. The great thirst for justice and equality in our America has led to the election of several more progressive presidents who symbolize the possibility of a future we all deserve. Our active participation, as Afro-Latinas, is the guarantee that racial matters will not be excluded from this process of repairing the historic exclusion of our people.

Black Girls Ride Tricycles Too
Thoughts from the Identities of an
Afro-descendent and Feminist Woman

ANA IRMA RIVERA LASSÉN

I AM FIFTY-FOUR YEARS OLD. I LOOK AT MYSELF IN THE MIRROR, see my short graying hair, and I still cannot believe that so much time has passed so quickly since the day I told myself that I would fight to prove to everyone that we women can do whatever we want to do. I made that promise to myself one day on the balcony of my house, a balcony too high for a four-year-old girl to see over. I used to look through the spaces at the bottom of the balcony wall, barely seeing the legs and feet of people passing by.

My mother had told me that the tricycle I wanted could not be mine because I was a girl. Those words stabbed me in the center of my being. I knew there was something wrong with that, something that pushed me to make myself that promise.

The memories of the feminist thoughts of my childhood blend with my memories of the mirror, always the mirror. It reflected the image of a black girl, myself, growing up with the imposition of white aesthetics and the pressures of a traditional upbringing for a girl, but at the same time with certain freedom of thought and a privileged access to books and information. The day we see our face in a mirror for the first time, with

67

a consciousness of self, we see a face, we see eyes, we see a
mouth, we see hair and skin. We make a judgment; we like or
dislike what we see. We may or may not want it to be another way, we feel that others like it or not, we accept it or we do
not, and in the end, we love it or not, as we love our own self.
Without going into a psychological analysis, that narcissistic
experience brings with it, for a black person, the acceptance or
rejection of a reflection laced with social judgments. The
blackness of our skin, the kinkiness of our hair, the width of
our nose and the thickness of our lips have meanings that go
beyond aesthetics; they also have economic, political and
social implications.[1]

At the age of sixteen, I started to keep my childhood
promise. I joined with other women to form the group Mujer
Intégrate Ahora, MIA (Woman Integrate Now) in 1972 in
Puerto Rico. As an adolescent, with the face of a girl but the
will of a woman, with an afro and skin that was obviously
black, I began to expose myself to the world wearing only my
utopias. My black girl's face started to become known long
before I had learned to know myself and the complexity of the
intersections of my being. Since then, I have thought a lot
about the activism that has marked so many years of my life.
Today I want to rethink it from my skin.

From the beginning of the activist movements of the
1970s in Puerto Rico, there has been tension between race
and feminism. When the first black women's organization was
founded in 1992, I thought even more about the invisibility of
the theme of race in feminist organizations throughout the
years. I don't mean that the faces of Puerto Rican feminists
have been white and insensitive to racial prejudice. The real-

---

[1] This essay is based on "Narciso, Zenón y la poesía: Mi reflejo en el espejo," a paper I presented at the Puerto Rican Studies Association (PRSA),
Ithaca, N.Y., 2006.

ity is that the faces of the women who have spoken publicly on behalf of independent feminist organizations throughout the years have been black, mulatto and white.[2]

The problem is not the image; it is the content of the discourse. We have been speaking about women from different perspectives and variations of the problems that affect us. The gender discourse in Puerto Rico has included reproductive rights, domestic violence, AIDS, sexual harassment, bisexuality, lesbianism, lesbophobia and women's health, among others. However, the relationship between race and gender, and the specificity of the related prejudice, has not been as large a part of our agendas as it should have throughout the years.

As I have said, our public image has been racially diverse, and although this is a positive expression in itself—after all, people do get to see black faces among the public speakers denouncing violence and discrimination against women—it is not enough, since it does not link the specific experience of black women to the general discourse. Black and mulatto women must claim not only the voice of the discourse, but also its content. It is not just who speaks that is relevant; what is being said is just as important.

Lesbian organizations have successfully brought lesbian issues into the feminist agenda. They declared that they would embrace their lesbianism, gather as lesbians and claim a space at the table in feminist organizations. According to my work in *El otro clóset*, they came out of the closet and brought out with them all the years of labor that they had spent in silence in feminist organizations, all the years of not mentioning the word "lesbian" so as not to frighten men, other women and the masses, and all sorts of other excuses given so that the organizations would not have to recognize their lesbophobia.

---

[2] Rivera Lassén, Ana Irma. (1995). *El otro clóset*, special magazine, *Fempress*. Santiago, Chile.

Afro-descendent women are also in our own closet. To come out of it, we must gather, discuss and organize ourselves. According to El otro clóset, our particular space in the feminist work we have been doing, and in the feminist work that still remains to be done, is a specter whose face we still do not recognize fully, although we feel it in the skin. If, in addition, we are also lesbians, then the challenge is even more complex.

In the 1970s, in Puerto Rico, there was great discussion concerning racism. One of the catalysts for that discussion was the publication of the book Narciso descubre su trasero (Narcissus discovers his behind) by Isabelo Zenón Cruz[3]. Volume I of the book was published in 1974, and the second volume followed in 1975, more than thirty years ago. Afros were fashionable at the time, and many blacks rediscovered themselves in their blackness. In that environment, Narciso immediately became a best seller. "Black is beautiful" was also the motto in Puerto Rico in those days, but Zenón, the author, shouted out that "Black is also Puerto Rican."[4] Professor Zenón challenged me to incorporate race in my feminist activism much more prominently. We spoke about the rights of black women and about sexual orientation as well. In those days, we did not call the phenomenon "intersections," but that is what we were talking about. Questioning myself was not a strange activity to me because, in theory, and more or less in practice, I was trying to bring to the fore those intersections.

I identified myself with Professor Zenón's ideas because he was also outside the most conservative and exclusionist nationalistic discourses. I understood what he was talking about because we feminists of that era were being accused of importing foreign ideas, ideas that were not really Puerto Rican, according to our accusers.

---

[3] Cruz, Isabelo Zenón. (1974). Narciso Descubre su Trasero, El Negro en la Cultura Puertorriqueña. Vol. I. Humacao, Puerto Rico: Editorial Furidi.

[4] Rivera Lassén, Ana. "Narciso, Zenón y la poesía: Mi reflejo en el espejo."

The same thing that had happened with the feminist discourse was happening with the discourse about racial prejudice: it was said that such discussions were foreign. Many people alleged that there was no such thing as racism in Puerto Rico because all Puerto Ricans were of mixed race. Others saw the discourse as imported from the exterior, as if the problem and the discussion were irrelevant to the Puerto Rican reality.

I wrote a poem for the second volume of Zenón's book, which rescued the image of the African character "Tembandumba" from the poetry of Luis Pales Matos and questioned the stereotypical images of Afro-descendent women and men displayed in the poet's verses. This poem is often printed and anthologized.[5]

One of the first bitter experiences I suffered as a spokesperson for the organization I belonged to, MIA, was related to racial prejudice. One day, a classmate at the University of Puerto Rico told me that his mother had seen me on TV and commented that I did not speak for her when I defended the rights of women. He asked her what she meant by that and was shocked to hear her reply: I did not represent her because I was black.

On the one hand, she was correct, since no one can claim to represent all women. But on the other, she was expressing a racist point of view that prevented her from seeing me as a person beyond the color of my skin. As a result, I learned that what nowadays we refer to as "intersections" is always present, that there is no such thing as the image of a "neutral" woman.

In the 1970s, in feminist groups, there were rarely any discussions about black or Afro-descendent women. Certainly, there was a rejection of racism in these organizations, but the issue of racism was not part of the agenda. I personally partic-

[5] Cruz, Isabelo Zenón. (1975). *Narciso Descubre su Trasero, El Negro en la Cultura Puertorriqueña.* Vol. II. Humacao, Puerto Rico: Editorial Furidi.

ipated as a representative of MIA in panels and activities that addressed racial prejudice and black women, but that was more my personal agenda than that of the organization.

However, MIA and the publication *El tacón de la chancleta* (The slipper's high heel), did theoretically bring up the need to address within the feminist discourse race, class, sexual orientation and other issues that provoked prejudice and discrimination. We affirmed that women suffered from all of these prejudices, but that our experience was different from that of men, that there had to be a recognition of that difference in order to understand it, and that the knowledge about these issues made feminism an indispensable political movement.

There were other Puerto Rican voices in that era that spoke out about the need to incorporate the issues of sexism and racism, as in the writings of journalist Eneid Routte Gómez. I had many long conversations with her about racial prejudice in Puerto Rico and the particular way in which women experienced it. Today I owe her so much for helping me articulate a coherent and holistic discourse that comes from my own intersections.

In the 1980s, other voices emerged, such as that of Marie Ramos Rosado, who addressed racial prejudice with an agenda centered specifically on the issues of black/Afro-descendent women. It was not until the 1990s that organizations appeared that specifically addressed the reality of Afro-descendent women. Among them are the Unión de Mujeres Puertorriqueñas Negras (UMUPUEN, Union of Black Puerto Rican Women) and the Grupo Identidad de la Mujer Negra (Group of Black Women's Identity), organizations that most of the time remain at the periphery of the activities of feminist organizations, even though many of us feminist women were instrumental in their creation. In 1992, we also participated, at the regional level, in the creation of the Red de Mujeres Afrocaribeñas y Afrolatinoamericanas (Network of Afro-

Caribbean and Afro–Latin American Women), now also including Afro-descendent women of the diaspora.

Feminisms do not necessarily attract all women who identify with the discussions about Afro-descendent women. Feminist organizations have, to some degree, begun to address the issue of race in their agendas and activities.[6] The tensions between feminist and Afro-descendent movements continue to exist; they are knots that all of us must continually work to unravel.

As part of our transversal analysis, we must recognize the multiplicity of identities that form part of our identity as women. I am all the identities at the same time; I am the intersection of all of them. We are all people with a nationality, race, ethnicity, sexual orientation and other identities all together. We do not leave any of our identities behind when we participate in an activity. However, that is exactly what analyses that do not recognize the transversality of identities try to do: they emphasize some identities at the expense of others. When we do that we become women with multiple personalities who cannot live with all of our identities at the same time, and, consequently, some of them will live in the closet.[7]

In the events known as the "Route to the United Nations," there was a great richness and diversity of organizations and women who came together to make their voices heard. I will always remember fondly when I was chosen to speak on behalf of the Caucus of NGO Women at the Conference of the Americas in Santiago, Chile, in 2000, a preparatory meeting leading up to the World Conference against Racism

---

[6] Rivera Lassén, Ana Irma. (2001). "La organización de las mujeres y las organizaciones feministas en Puerto Rico: Mujer Intégrate Ahora y otras historias de la década." In Ana Irma Rivera Lassén and Elizabeth Crespo Kebler, Documentos del feminismo en Puerto Rico: Facsímiles de la historia, vol. I, 1970–79. San Juan: Editorial Universidad de Puerto Rico.

[7] Rivera Lassén, Ana Irma. (2003). "Memoria Foro Internacional Las Mujeres en el siglo XXI." In Mujeres de dos siglos: lecturas cruzadas y categorías cambiantes. La Paz, Bolivia: Edición CIDEM.

of 2001. I spoke of myself as an Afro-descendent person: I am a person of the Caribbean, a region that enjoys the great diversity of the whole Western Hemisphere; a region that is multiracial, multicultural, multilinguistic; a region that also has a wide geopolitical diversity, with independent as well as non-independent countries; and a region that also includes a socialist country. When we talk about the intersections between gender, race and other forms of discrimination, we must also include geopolitical diversity.

In those days, Puerto Ricans were struggling to expel the U.S. Navy from the island of Vieques, which was also a good opportunity to bring up many of our claims. At the Conference of the Americas, I explained that at the World Conference against Racism we needed to link our experience to the experience of women living in countries in conflict around the world, and how conflict affects displaced women in particular. This was happening in the Caribbean as well. The North Atlantic Treaty Organization (NATO) and the United States were conducting war games using live ammunition in Vieques, Puerto Rico. The women of Vieques suffered many of the same problems that displaced women in conflict zones were experiencing elsewhere. This situation could only be made visible if 1) Puerto Rico, which has no representation in the United Nations, had the opportunity to be heard, 2) the activities of the U.S. Marines were exposed as racist and discriminatory and 3) if we could establish a link to gender issues.

Women in non-independent countries (countries subject to an administrator state) must be included in discussions at world forums. Our voices must be heard along with those of other women who do not want to remain silenced and invisible. This is what happens to us when women are not even mentioned at all or when discussions fail to use a gender perspective.

The Caucus of NGO Women wanted to ensure that when representatives of nations spoke at the conference about the commitments made through international conventions, treaties and conferences, the interlinks were made in order to see the true dimensions of women's reality. We wanted the content of the documents coming out of the conference to reflect the face, the color, the suffering, the resistance, the strength and the hope of all women and men. We wanted an exercise in the intersections with gender issues, with the issues of indigenous peoples and nations and Afro-descendents, migrants, displaced people, disabled people and victims of xenophobia, homophobia and other hate crimes. We wanted a plan of action to come out of the conference that would begin with the collection of national population census data, which would include the categories of race, ethnicity and language, and continue with affirmative action plans and human rights education plans that would promote human sexuality, gender equality and cultural diversity.

Our participation in and deliberations at UN conferences cannot be our only drive. They can help us see where our governments are headed and where they are not. The power of our organizations and movements comes from keeping the necessary distance from the state apparatus, maintaining a position that is committed to change, free enough to see and strong enough to demand. We must remain independent enough to be able to see reality and demand change. I have reflected here on the past because, in order to continue our march ahead, we sometimes need to stop and examine the path, not the path ahead, but the path we have left behind. I conclude these thoughts with an allegory.

The horizon is the icon of the utopias that we aspire to reach someday. It is the line in the distance toward which we move. However, as we advance toward it, the horizon is not closer, it remains there in the distance. The horizon, just like utopias, is always present and is always distant. Our gains are the steps on our paths and our footprints are our legacies, the paths made of our dreams. After we have taken all those steps and think we have arrived, we realize that we have a new perspective of the horizon that we had not seen before. This is the larger challenge, not to resign ourselves with the steps already taken, but to learn from our stumbles and continue walking, knowing that the very nature of utopias is the permanent rebelliousness of not being canon nor norm. We must have the will to reinvent ourselves at each step of the way, our identity being the horizon.[8]

---

[8] Translation of this chapter was provided by Elizabeth Crespo Kebler.

Afro-Boricua: Nuyorican de Pura Cepa

MARTA MORENO VEGA

THE BLACK AND WHITE DIALOGUE ON RACE AND CULTURE IN the United States has consistently ignored the existence of more than 150 million people of African ancestry in the other Americas. The total absence of Afro-Latinas/os from the Caribbean, Mexico, Central America and South America in the consciousness of the national discourse in the United States, including in institutions that educate and inform the civil society of the nation, contributes to the absolute disregard of the presence and realities of African diasporic communities within the U.S. national territory and abroad. This lack of recognition and omission of the history, contributions and lives of more than 150 million people of African ancestry, many of whom reside here in the United States, renders their contributions and lives irrelevant. For those of us who are the first generation born here, of parents who immigrated to the United States as a result of this country's intervention in the political and economic structures of their once sovereign countries, we are still in the process of understanding and constructing our racial and cultural presence in the clock of history. This leads me to conclude that I am a work in progress.

I am an Afro-Boricua born in New York's El Barrio; I am "Nuyorican de pura cepa."[1] I know that my racial and cultural identities will continue to evolve as the image of myself continues to change, and as I learn more about our peoples' journey before and after enslavement: lessons of the philosophical, spiritual and living practices that have contributed to constructing a thinking and a day-to-day existence infused with racial, cultural and ancestral sacred thought. Like pieces of a puzzle coming together, I have had the opportunity to witness the lives of my communities in different countries. This has instilled in me a depth of understanding, of realizing how much we do not know about our past, how that lack of knowledge defines who we are as Afro-descendents and how much we need to do to try to capture this knowledge and understanding, which are integral and vibrant to our people. The Quilombos of Brazil, the Palenques of Colombia and the remnants of maroon communities in Puerto Rico, Cuba and other locations are spaces of African affirmation. They are living narratives of our victories against, and continued resistance to, cultural oppression by Eurocentric cultural and policy practices that are still dominant in our countries. The images and identities others project on to me contribute to a kaleidoscope of revolving understandings that are sometimes curious intrusions and enlightening revelations as I continue the journey of grasping my experience. I am, therefore, still in the process of becoming.

Experiencing my brothers and sisters from Nicaragua, Costa Rica, Uruguay, Cuba and other locations further opens both my internal and external dialogue. This dialogue requires

---

[1] A Nuyorican *de pura cepa* is a Puerto Rican born in New York. In *From Colonia to Community: The History of Puerto Ricans in New York City* (Berkeley: U of California P, 1983), Virginia E. Sánchez Korrol indicates the presence of Puerto Ricans in New York early in the 1800s.

a constant revision that contributes to my increased knowledge of the historical and contemporary complexities that factor into the way I see myself clearly within a global context. As ripples that travel across the ocean, the diasporic communities that are part of my life seamlessly reflect who I am now and who I am still becoming. I know that the flow of experiences provides *caminos*, roads of new information, that will always create change and simultaneously provide a sense of completion. As the familiar phrase notes, the more we know, the more we realize how much more there is to know. Additionally, new information often leads us to redefine, reconstruct and view what we understood from varying perspectives.

The World Conference against Racism, which was organized by the United Nations in Durban, South Africa, in 2001, was one of those transformative experiences that led me to better understand how I am viewed by the nation that colonized Puerto Rico, the island of my parents' birth, and my reality as a Puerto Rican/Nuyorican woman of African ancestry who was born in the United States. During the conference, European countries, together with the United States, were intransigent about apologizing for the enslavement of Africans as a result of the Atlantic slave trade and refused to consider reparations. As reported in *The Observer* on September 9, 2001, by Chris McGreal in Durban, the final wording of the declaration, adopted by the European Union at the conference, reflected the position primarily proposed by the British, which fell far from an apology: "We acknowledge that slavery and the slave trade, including the trans-Atlantic slave trade, were appalling tragedies in the history of humanity, not only because of their abhorrent barbarism, but also in terms of their magnitude, organized nature and especially their negation of the essence of victims. . . ."

The Europeans also won on their insistence that only modern slavery can be called a crime against humanity

because the trans-Atlantic slave trade was legal at the time.[2]
The circumventing language that made no direct reference to
the culpability of European countries and the United States
was further made absolutely clear when the United States
walked out of the conference, claiming that the United
Nations document was racist against Israel. According to
CNN.com/World, the United States and Israel walked out of
the UN conference because it had been hijacked by Israel's
enemies. The European Union also made clear the language
was unacceptable.[3]

A broad representation of African and African diasporic
communities went to Durban to discuss the destructive impact
of racism and discrimination within their countries and also to
address the need for an apology by European countries, the
United States and other countries that participated in the
slave trade. It was obvious during the conference that the
power still remains with Europe and the United States, as they
obviously dominated the proceedings. The United States and
European nations led by the British still were able to block discussions of equity and reparations. Slave-trading nations that
included Holland, Spain and Portugal objected to the word
apology because, according to McGreal's report in *The Observer*, use of that word would provide legal grounds for future law-
suits. In addition to walking out and later leaving a lame and
absent representative, the United States refused to meet with
very diverse racial and cultural groups from the United States
that requested a meeting and an explanation of their nation's
position against declaring the slave trade a crime against
humanity.

---

[2] The enslavement of Africans and their descendents ended in the British
Empire in 1833 and in the United States in 1865.
[3] See "U.S. Disappointed, Others Pleased," CNN.com September 6, 2001:
http://archives.cnn.com/WORLD/africa/09/08/racism.agree.reaction/index.
html.

Attending the conference forced me to face certain realities that, up to that point, I had refused to accept fully: racism and discriminatory practices are inextricably linked to economic global profit and domination. Institutions or groups with different morality or ethical practices, and that oppose this global marketing approach, will continue to be suppressed.

In light of this reality, it is curious, and yet understandable, that the governments of Britain and the United States are preparing to commemorate the end of enslavement in their countries. The planned commemoration was scheduled to happen in 2007 or 2008—an illusion supported by UNESCO, believable only by those who don't have the historical facts. The reality is that enslavement persisted through the involvement of these two countries well into the end of the nineteenth century. How this clandestine process of enslavement enriched Britain and the United States, and disenfranchised and oppressed the lives of Africans and their descendents, is virtually ignored. Rather than commemorating the inhumane treatment of Africans that should not have occurred in the first place, Britain and the United States should be at the forefront of constructing and implementing global methods of reparations to Africans in Africa and in the Americas. Much is owed, and special events do little to rectify the ravages of centuries of enforced economic deprivation. If we look at the actions of Britain and the United States at the World Conference against World Racism, it is clear why they would support a commemoration. These countries are patting themselves on the back for eliminating horrendous practices that should have never been acceptable. *These* were crimes against humanity.

The historian, Joseph C. Dorsey, addresses the continued enslavement of Africans by Britain and the United States after the official abolition of slavery in his book *Slave Traffic in the Age of Abolition in Puerto Rico, West Africa and the Non-*

Hispanic Caribbean, 1815–1859 (Gainesville: University Press of Florida, 2003). According to Dorsey, "The shift from legal to illegal slave trading rendered the 1820s a period of trial and error. At some levels, however, tradition is difficult to discern. The organization of transport not only remained in the hands of multinational fortune hunters, but British efforts failed to curb the activities of slave-trading firms. Until the 1850s, these firms continued to disguise themselves as French, Spanish and Portuguese shipping companies with branch offices in Cuba, Puerto Rico, the United States and England itself" (3).

The myths that fuel celebrations, that honor misinformation, continue to cloud the devastating impact of the enslavement of more than 15 million Africans over a period of more than four hundred years. The legacy of racism and economic marginality, which has devastated the lives of more than 150 million African descendents, remains hidden. Misinformation, coupled with miseducation, continues to "color" how we are perceived by others and the lenses we use to view ourselves.

I am a product of the failing public schools of New York City. In high school I was fortunate to be admitted into a "specialized high-achieving academic high school" that made me aware that my previous elementary and middle school education was designed to fail young people like me. I thought that this was particular to the United States, where segregation, our version of apartheid, had developed a dual educational school system based on color that was separate and unequal. The opportunity to connect with my global community has demonstrated that wherever critical masses of African descendents are, the support services provided by government are basically lacking. Health care is rare, educational opportunities are extremely limited, job opportunities are almost non-existent, housing conditions are the worst and issues of land rights and displacement from fertile and mineral rich lands are all persistent forces undermining the livelihoods of African descendents.

The CRS Report for Congress entitled "Afro-Latinos in Latin America and Considerations of U.S. Policy" states the following: "Afro-Latinos comprise some 150 million of the region's 540 million total population, and, along with women and indigenous populations are among the poorest, most marginalized groups in the region. Afro-Latinos have begun forming groups that, with the help of international organizations, are seeking political representation, human rights protection, land rights and greater social and economic rights and benefits."[4]

The primary vehicle for affirming racist and discriminatory theories and practices is the educational system of our countries. The historical narratives that generally frame our experience start solely with our enslavement. The general absence of our pre-enslavement and post-enslavement history is a major factor in determining the information we use to define our individual and group identities. Mis-education still continues to frame a world that questions the validity of my existence as an Afro-Boricua-Nuyorican. Sojourner Truth, an enslaved woman who became an abolitionist and freed many enslaved Africans, posed the question in a public speech that challenged the definition and role of a woman: "Ain't I a woman?" Her speech delivered in 1851 still resonates in the lives of women who are descendents of Africans. I ask myself, am I a black woman? Am I Latina? Am I a mulata? Am I black enough because I am also Latina? Am I Latina if I was born in New York? Am I Puerto Rican if I was not born on the island? Who determines?

Long ago I decided to define how I planned to construct the world I wish to live in. The mother of two sons, I was

---

[4] See Ribando, Clare. (January 4, 2005). "Afro-Latinos in Latin America and Considerations of U.S. Policy."

determined to provide a nurturing environment and create
institutions that would reflect who my sons are within their
communities and in the world. If there is a point that clearly
marks my self-identification as a person who is actively
involved in living in the struggle for racial and social justice,
it is the birth of my first son, Sergio, and five years later the
birth of my son, Omar. My sons to me are a reflection of the
young people, the students who are in my classes. These young
people are seeking to connect to their historical pasts, to
understand the challenges they face, which in a just environment would not be issues. My sons are routinely stopped by
police and frisked because they are Afro–Puerto Ricans. This
happens to most young men who are of African ancestry: it is
not an exception, it is the rule. As a mother I live with the
fear, as do other mothers, of having my children falsely incar-
cerated or randomly shot by mistake. Why must we, as parents, daily fear for the lives of our young?

The motivating principle, that has driven my involvement
in building institutions and organizations, is the desire to create safe spaces for our communities that are cultural and educational oases, that are urban *palenques* and *quilombos*.[5] The
Caribbean Cultural Center African Diaspora Institute, which
I founded in 1976, was designed to be an institution where our
community scholars, traditional leaders, academics and community members could gather to share information in diverse
areas of interest.

In keeping with the concept of creating a global village for
our young, my sons and now my granddaughter, Kiya, and my
nieces and nephews, has become the spark that continues to
regenerate and invigorate ideas that spread beyond familial
borders to all of our communities. The warrior women who

---

[5] *Palenques* and *quilombos* refer to "towns" established in inaccessible areas
by runaway enslaved Africans in Latin America and the Caribbean.

have made a difference in our communities have consistently maintained a familial, culturally grounded construct to build upon that is infused with ancestral sacred beliefs that honor family, friends, network, community, humanity and the universality of our experiences.

Since our communities have historically been and continue to be under siege, it is critical for us to have safe spaces. The opportunity to learn and share research, in an encouraging and challenging environment, enriches our communities and provides a stable learning process guided by educators, curators, scholars and traditional and community experts who are immersed in their subject areas. The international gathering of our experts and interactions with our international African diasporic communities has provided the documentation, the historical analysis and the educational lenses with which we can view ourselves.

The changing and projected images of others remain a curious intrusion in the images I have of myself. I peel away the layers of mis-education and construct my own lenses that are culturally grounded on information shared by scholars and traditional leaders, who are committed to rectifying misinformation and exploring new areas of study too long ignored and marginalized. This process has led to the building of institutions that are urban replications of ancient *quilombos* and *palenques* built on principles of racial and social justice. This process has made me revise and confront both my internal and external dialogues. Work regarding the international African diaspora has helped me connect El Barrio of New York to those barrios of Brazil, Colombia, Venezuela, Argentina, Uruguay and other countries that are home to those who honor their African ancestry. Ribando, in her introduction to the CRS Report for Congress, mentioned above, observes that "improvement in the status of Afro-Latinos could be difficult and contentious, however, depending on the size and circum-

stances of the African descent populations of each country." It
is my position that our work, as people of African ancestry, is
to confront the barriers that continue to marginalize our existence by building community and grounded institutions to
reinforce our efforts at local, national and international
forums. Making our issues an international effort is essential.
There is no question that the local efforts, in our case, are also
international in scope.

I learned in school that El Barrio, the community of my
birth, was a ghetto. In reality, it was a community that reflected the diversity of its residents' experiences as Puerto Ricans,
Caribbeans and African Americans. Economically poor, yet
rich in cultural traditions, El Barrio in New York was a *quilombo*, teaching the young about their cultural traditions. Now
that land in New York City is at a premium, the communities
of my birth are being displaced by wealthy landowners who are
building high-rise condominiums for the wealthy. This scenario is replicated in culturally rich African diasporic communities that live in ancestral lands, which are desired by multinational corporations for international tourism by the wealthy.

Today, the people of Piñones, Puerto Rico, a historically
Afro-descendent area, are fighting to keep multinational corporations from gentrifying their communities. In Choco, Colombia's African descendents are struggling to maintain their min-
eral-rich lands; the children of maroons in Brazil are fighting to
save their *quilombos*, their historically liberated lands.

At this point in my life's journey, the deepening connection with the global sisterhood and brotherhood of African
descendents has helped me understand how thoroughly
ingrained and universal the constructs of racism and discriminatory systems are currently. Reflecting on the outcome of the
World Conference against World Racism of 2001, and on the
historical roles and present positions of countries that profited

from the enslavement of Africans and their descendents, I conclude that there is still much to do to overturn these constructs.

How valiant and powerful are the spirit and will we possess, as a people, to assure our place in the world? Be they in
the tenements of El Barrio in New York, or *favelas* (shanty-
towns) of Brazil, or the improvised rural farms of the Dominican Republic, the will and heroism of African descendents to
confront oppression is relentless and powerful. The challenges
we confront are located within our own communities, as well
as outside our communities at the national and international
levels. The lessons from my local community become the
practices I incorporate into my international work.

When I was a little girl, my loving father called me his
negrita, his little black one, a term of endearment to remind me
that I was black and loved. One day Lupe, a friend of my mother, asked her, "How is it that you daughter is *tan negrita?*" She
spoke in a tone registering astonishment. Without missing a
beat, my mother responded, *"Ella tiene que ser negrita porque su
papá es negro y yo con mi piel clara soy una negra jaba como tú"*
(She has to be black because her father is black and, although
I have a light skin color, I am a light-skinned black like you).
The woman's face froze. With a sharp dismissive huff, my
mother turned away from her friend, took my hand and left
without saying another word. I knew from my mother's silence
and stern expression not to ask why we left so abruptly, but I
knew that it had something to do with my being *negrita* and my
family being *negros*. I did wonder why my mother kept calling
herself *negra*, since she was much lighter than my father, my
brother and I, and everyone thought of her as *blanca* as they did
my light-skinned *jaba* sister. After we had walked a short distance, my mother said, "Never be afraid of speaking the truth.
When you allow people to speak *mentiras* [untruths] and they
go unchallenged, they believe untruths to be the truth—*las
mentiras se convierten en la verdad.*" Without a doubt, my moth-

er taught me to be present in my life and that of my family and community. Her teachings are part of my DNA.

The flood of experiences that have created who I am reflect the ancestral experiences that have been embedded in the memory of my soul. The transatlantic journey of my ancestors from Africa to Puerto Rico, and the generations I never met because there are no records that identify them, are waiting for me to find a means of accessing them. My paternal grandmother would recall memories the more her aged eyes lost their sight. She spoke about a past, through her spiritual guides, in ways that my young mind could not understand. My parents provided lessons on love and resistance daily as they worked hard to hold their family together, all the while protecting us against racism, even as they practiced racist forms of love to protect us—*mi negrita linda* (my pretty little black girl).

My parents created a life outside of their homeland: they were refugees in the land that colonized and disenchanted their island. The trauma of having been forced to learn English in Puerto Rico caused my mother to refuse to speak English in her new home, New York City. My father came to New York with a third-grade education and the skill of having been a carpenter's apprentice. My mother came with a high school diploma and the desire to become a nurse. Both of my parents came to El Barrio—the section of New York that had recreated Puerto Rico in the sea of gray tenement buildings and storefront *bodegas*, *botánicas* and home-grown churches—in search of greater opportunity. My parents met in El Barrio and grew old together in it, refusing to leave the area that was their Puerto Rico, their *quilombo*.

Our family was protected by the ancestral spirits of my grandmother, Abuela Luisa, who was born in Loiza Aldea, Puerto Rico. She had rich chocolate skin and smelled of tobacco; using Florida water, she would call on the Congo and Yoruba spirits of Africa whenever a problem needed to be

solved for the family. When a problem arose during my childhood, she would always assure me that the warrior Congo's
spirit walked with me and would always form a protective
shield around me. When I went to Cuba for my doctoral
research, the spiritists of Cuba would see and remind me of the
spirits that protected me.

My parents' private kitchen conversations after they put
my siblings and me to bed, which we were not supposed to
hear, let us know what awaited us in our adulthood. Papi spoke
of how his color and language were ridiculed by fellow workers, how he quit when the boss short-changed his paycheck.
He had no legal standing, since he was off the books. We felt
the pain in Papi's voice as he fought to keep his pride intact
while it was under constant assault by outsiders and to remain
the man of the house and retain the love and respect of his
wife. We heard the quivering hurt and fright in Mami's voice
as she wondered how the rent would be paid and tried to figure out how long the money in hand would last. We were not
supposed to hear, but we did. I felt the surge of fear cover me
like a cold blanket. Abuela said the spirits would always provide and they did.

My family name is absolutely appropriate and fits me
because it describes me. *Moreno/a* means dark. My father was
un moreno, a strapping proud tall black man born in Puerto
Rico. A man of *su palabra*, of his word, he struggled to find a
space in New York during the late 1920s, when little was
known about Puerto Ricans, much less Puerto Ricans of
African descent. I was raised on the stories of how white workers did not allow him to work on carpentry machines in New
York, the trade he had learned in Puerto Rico. The only job
offers he received were to sweep the factory after hours. With
a steady, strong voice to hide the pain he would say, "*Soy un
hombre. No es justo que me traten menos porque soy negro*" (I am
a man. It isn't right that they treat me as less because I am

black). He changed his trade and became a body and fender auto worker who fixed mangled cars. Exhausted when he walked into our home, he would always want an update from Mami on *los negritos*.

My mother, light skinned, tall and strong, had features that spoke of her father's ebony skin and her mother's light complexion. She took great care making sure that her two daughters' nappy hair would be soft and shiny, using coconut oil and braiding it tightly to give the impression that we almost had "good hair." We were always neatly dressed to teach *la gente* —other people, generally whites or light-skinned Puerto Ricans— that to be black was not to be dirty and poorly dressed. My parents were clear that their children would study and become professionals so that our intelligence would not be questioned because of our blackness. The message was clear: To be black and Puerto Rican was to live a life of enduring tests.

We heard how my father quit many jobs because he was disrespected. His color and his accent were barriers to finding a job "on the books." When he was hired on the books, he was underpaid and was hired short term. He refused to be bent by the obstacles he faced, convinced that his skills, hard work and dedication to his employers would one day earn him the money to provide adequately for his family. My father would not allow my mother to work. Her job was to care for our home and us. Although her salary would have helped pay bills that constantly went unpaid, she could not work since it would send the message that my father could not provide for his family.

In the 1940s, one of the yardsticks that defined a man as a man was his ability to provide for his family. The women, having married well, were defined by being able to stay home to raise their children. Both of my parents worked hard to provide a safe space for their children and hoped that we would fulfill dreams they could not. Their hopes were defined by their educational, social and economic circumstances. Their dreams deferred became the dreams of their children.

My parents gave us love, moral values, ethics and humanity without acknowledging them as activism and passion for righting wrongs. To be actively involved in righting whatever is wrong was a responsibility my parents instilled. The mantra in my house was *"Tú no eres mejor que nadie y nadie es mejor que tú"* (You are not better than anyone and no one is better than you). They contradicted this when it came to African descendents that did not speak Spanish. Somehow speaking Spanish made us better.

My housewife mother turned into a raging warrior woman when the principal of my elementary school questioned whether her daughter, and the children of my public school, had the intelligence to pass a citywide test. She attacked him with words that pierced like a sharp sword: If the other students and I failed the test it was due to the lack of quality teachers and their lack of expectations for us. She reminded him in her broken English that Puerto Ricans are not foreigners; we were citizens because of the U.S. invasion of Puerto Rico and the Jones Act of 1917, which imposed U.S. citizenship on Puerto Ricans. Without understanding the political implications of her statement, I, as a nine-year-old, did understand that my mother was afraid of no one, that her children were precious and that she would protect us at all cost.

I now know that to be Afro-Boricua is to be an activist and revolutionary by birth. It is not a choice: it is a birth-right that insists that your existence be acknowledged, your intelligence praised, your space respected, your voice heard, your color not questioned, your gender honored and your physicality embraced. We must assume the sovereignty of our existence as we seek the independence of our parents' homeland. As their children defining their right to their island, we also claim our geographic heritage and place on the planet.

Since the occupation of Puerto Rico by the United States in 1898, making the island its possession, the overt destruction of what is Puerto Rican has been relentless. With the colonizers came the mission of Americanization, and a primary vehicle used was the Protestant church. The island was divided into nine sectors, allowing the different branches of Protestantism to have a section of the island to convert. My mother went to school on the island during the time that American teachers, who had been trained to destroy Native American cultures in the United States, went to Puerto Rico to do the same.

English was the language of instruction in Puerto Rico. The traumatic experience of being taught in English caused my mother to refuse to speak English because it violated her right to her language and existence as a Puerto Rican. My parents instilled in my siblings and me the idea that to be Puerto Rican was our right. Another mantra was *"Ustedes son negros puertorriqueños"* (You are black Puerto Ricans). When my African American friends challenged my blackness, my parents would point to our color saying, *"Si no son negros ¿qué son?"* (If you are not black then what are you?).

These were the driving words that motivated my interest in the history and culture of Puerto Rico in order to understand who I am. As part of that process, it was necessary to place Puerto Rico in the history of the Caribbean, Central America, South America and North America. Without question, the contextualization of my racial and cultural identity required connecting to Africa and the Americas as a product of the African diaspora brought about by the transatlantic slave trade.

The transforming civil rights movement of the 1950s and 1960s, and the Black Power movement that followed it through the early 1980s, were and continue to be the living texts of my self-realization, through which I understand the country in which I was born and the work that needs to be done to assure that my children and their children have better opportunities than those provided to those who came before us.

The images of water hoses forcing young black women, and men to the floor and of attack dogs ready to pounce on them, contrast with the faces of peaceful defiance of my brothers and sisters, who refused to ride buses that were symbols of the apartheid system functioning in the United States—these images became etched in my mind and penetrated my inner being. The question that resonated in my soul was, as an Afro–Puerto Rican young woman, what did the civil rights movement mean to me? My internal dialogue had to confront the racist and discriminatory teachings that I grew up with and confronted daily as an Afro-Boricua.

My parents made it clear that I was *negra*. They also made a clear distinction between being Puerto Rican and *negra,* and being an American English-speaking black. In their minds there was a difference. To be Puerto Rican and *negra* was better, even though discriminatory practices against *negros* are still very much part of the Spanish-speaking world. Phrases that speak to whiteness as the desired complexion are still part of daily conversations, reminding us of continued internal discriminatory practices. My Afro–Puerto Rican and Dominican students too often share stories of how their parents insist that they only date and marry a light-skinned person. A young student shared her story as she imitated her mother, "Marry someone whiter than you—advance the race! You want your children to have straight hair—good hair, not nappy bad hair." Squeezing her nose she said, "Make sure he has a straight nose." Many other students in class acknowledged that their parents felt the same way when it came to race issues. Although they laughed hearing the students' stories, a sadness quickly spread in the classroom.

There are endless variations on phrases that speak to white preference at the expense of being *negra*. Most unfortunate is that these phrases come out of our own mouths. I will always recall my mother's reaction to my marriage to my high-school sweetheart: "With his straight hair and your nappy hair, the children will have wavy hair." The contradiction of embracing Negritude, while still accepting the concept of "advancing the race," is an issue that we must confront as a community of African descendents.

The discussion of "shade-ocracy," a term I created to address our preoccupation with skin color and skin tones, too often neglects the importance of how African-derived traditional philosophies, belief systems and sacred practices, that are historically grounded in the heritages of West and Central Africa, affect contemporary society and our lives. These ancestral practices are integral to the lives of Afro-Latinas/os. The Eurocentric societies that we have grown up in have intentionally and consistently demonized our African traditions, terming them exotic, sinful and devil-like, and categorizing them as primitive, quaint and folkloric. In many instances, our countries undervalue our histories and practices, which reinforce our racial ancestry. The public faces of African traditions are ridiculed. In Argentina two years ago, I saw an advertisement for a package of toilet paper that was a cartoon of a black man smiling and showing sparkling white teeth that were compared to the rolls of toilet paper in the package. In Colombia, a television advertisement had a cartoon image of broad exaggerated lips and wide exaggerated eyes, obviously referring to a black man. In Cuba and Brazil, the bodies of Afro-descendent women are advertisements for cultural tourism, promoting overt sexuality and the exotic hot "mulata." In the United States, the image of Aunt Jemima on pancake cartons was updated from the robust Mammy stereo-

type associated with enslaved house servants to a more contemporary version of a maid.

The process of seeking to understand my image and those
of my family, my friends, my students and my community continues, while seeking to combat the negative public images
and texts that are supposed to reflect us. Today there is a growing international awareness, among African descendents, of
the need to publicly combat negative practices and point
them out to the global community and to international and
multinational organizations and governments. The international networking occurring among Afro-descendents, especially Afro-Latinas, speaks to possibilities that were not available to our parents. We are clear *"que en la unión está la fuerza"*:
transformative power lies in numbers and organized critical
thinking and creative communities, such as ours.

African descendents are internationalizing the issues of
our communities as we meet, recognize and see each other as
reflections of each other, and form networks and alliances to
address our common issues. We encounter the ancestral line-
age of our past in the faces that we see and in the voices that
we hear, as we wonder if we have reconnected to a family
member of our ancestral African village. It is in these encounters that change will be forged. It is in these encounters that I
will better understand who I am. It is in these encounters that
the stories I must share with my granddaughter will be learned.

Where the Heart Is: Family, Work and my Binational Life as a Black Brazilian Scholar

VÂNIA PENHA-LOPES[1]

I AM AN INTELLECTUAL. BEING AN INTELLECTUAL, WHEN ONE is a black woman from Brazil, does not come easily. While I may take my professional status for granted, there is a near-ly daily process of educating people about who I am and what it means to make a living out of reading, writing, teaching and delivering lectures. In that sense, I am an activist.

The practice of informing others about my place in the world is not particular to me. That is because, even after more than a century since the abolition of slavery in Brazil, it is still more common for people of African descent to be seen and not heard. Notwithstanding the voices clamoring for public policies that address racial injustice—and there are many—there are still many others who have been silenced by years of oppression and despair, and the need to carve out a living. At the same time, being an intellectual requires creating a space out of which it is legitimate to speak and be heard, to offer one's reflections to the world and be acknowledged as a worthy contributor.

---

[1] To the memory of Aglaís Pereira Oliveira (December 9, 1968–December 13, 2006), whose light was brutally turned off in the course of my writing this chapter. May she live on through her children and through our hearts, which she touched with every positive word that she uttered to each of us.

97

It is also more common for Afro-Brazilians to be studied, but not to study; in other words, to be a passive object rather than an active subject. Many an academic career has been established on the studies of every aspect of black life, particularly the Afro-Brazilian religions and other cultural manifestations. Traditionally, however, most of the students of Afro-Brazilian life have been white. Whites, by the way, have been left free to tackle whatever kind of research they fancy. When it comes to blacks being scholars, however, there is less reciprocity. They are either questioned on their competence to carry on their work in whatever area they choose or they are "encouraged" to confine their studies to other blacks. I ought to know. It happened to me over and again during my years as a graduate student in the United States.

None of that should sound new to blacks from other countries. Granted, perhaps because Brazil was the last country to abolish slavery (in 1888), its legacy of racial exclusion may appear rawer than that of other countries. Yet, because each country with a slave past practices some sort of racial exclusion, it is bound to erect barriers to black intellectuals. Such is the case, for example, of African American scholars. While their proportion is larger than in Brazil, they are still less represented among the tenured professors and the public intellectuals in the United States. In other words, they too often need to inform others of their place in the world.

I speak about these issues from experience. Having been born and raised in Rio de Janeiro, I was fortunate to have a family—especially a mother—who encouraged my lifelong dreams of being a scholar. After graduating from college, I won a national scholarship for study abroad and moved to the United States for graduate school. What was meant to be a year abroad turned out to be decades, to the point where I have now spent more time in the United States than in my native country. My Brazilian roots have called me back, however, and now I strive to live a bi-national life, living and working in both countries.

The process of living in two countries puts me in a privileged position to observe and experience major changes that have been taking place. I moved to the United States in the 1980s, right when the country was embarking on Reaganism. I have seen the United States become more and more conservative, to the point where the national climate after September 11 reminds me of aspects of the military dictatorship I had left behind in Brazil so many years earlier. I also first came to the United States having been inspired by the gains of the civil rights movement, only to see those gains being usurped. Conversely, having left Brazil as a dictatorship, I witnessed from the Northern Hemisphere its change to democracy. I have also seen Brazil bury its myth of racial democracy, acknowledge its racism (not, of course, without resistance), and address it with a much contested affirmative action program. In fact, it is the excitement of seeing history in the making that has encouraged me to spend a longer period of time in my own country.

I see myself as a black Brazilian. In the United States, however, my racial-ethnic identity is less apparent. Because of my lack of accent in English, people think of me as American until told otherwise; however, widespread ignorance about things Brazilian, especially the language we speak, makes most Americans think of me as Hispanic. Since I do not speak Spanish, I reject that label in favor of Latina. My race makes me, then, Afro-Latina, even though I only think in those terms when I am in the United States. As a sociologist, I know that the term "Latina" (or "Hispanic," for that matter) only really makes sense in the United States, a society with a palpable need to lump peoples into large categories and which wants to differentiate the immigrants from Central America and South America from "whites," the privileged racial group, and from blacks, the historically subordinate racial group. It is as if the people of the United States saw Latinos as a sort of intermediate "race," interstitially placed between whites and blacks. Also, like most Brazilians, when I hear the word "Latinos," I think of all those peoples who speak Romance languages and come from Mediterranean cultures, such as the Spanish, the Portuguese, the Italians and the French, in addition to Central and South Americans. Yet, in the United States, the Italians and the French are undoubtedly placed among whites and away from Latinos.

In any event, in both Brazil and the United States, it is obvious that it is my race that stands out. It is evident in the surprise on the faces of American students who are not used to having a black Brazilian woman professor; in the shock of many at my professional status ("I thought you were a student"); in the fear of the white Brazilian woman who acted as if she thought I was about to rob her when, like her, I wanted to use an ATM in Rio; and in the comments of a secretary at a Brazilian university who recently referred to me as "a girl" even though she had been introduced to me, more than once, as "a professor doctor."

Here I trace my trajectory as a Brazilian intellectual of African descent who lives and works in Brazil and the United States, from the time I decided to be a social scientist, as a teenager, to now, when I practice sociology. I also address questions pertaining to my sources of inspiration, my vision for Afro-Latina communities, the way I balance work and the other areas of my life, my challenges and accomplishments and my sources of regeneration.

Sources of Inspiration

A strong sense of family loyalty and pride keeps me inspired in pursuing my goals. In fact, my ancestors are my inspiration. Though I only knew two of my grandparents, I

learned a lot about my genealogy by having them answer my
constant questions from the time I was a little girl. I grew up
seeing Antonio Penha, my maternal grandfather, as my idol;
he remains so to this day. The son of a former slave, born but
six years after the abolition of slavery, he had very little formal
education, only three years, as is unfortunately still common
among Afro-Brazilians. Yet Vovô[2] was a visionary with his two
feet firmly planted on the ground. He was a school custodian
who loved books and possessed an elegant penmanship. He
fell in love with and married my grandmother, Levinda (who
died years before my mother got married and had children),
who, like him, was from the countryside and was believed to
know all about medicinal herbs and fruit trees. With his paid
work and her family work, they managed to acquire a relatively large piece of land in a Rio neighborhood (called, coinci-
dentally, Penha, like their family name), on which they raised
chickens and ducks, and planted a variety of tropical fruit
trees, which yielded avocados and bananas, coconuts and
guavas, oranges and papayas, *sapotis* and *pitangas* and so many
others. My mother is fond of telling the story of the way her
mother decided to plant mango trees so that they would grow
faster: by peeling the mango pits.

Vovó Levinda was known as a generous woman who liked
to share the fruits of her trees with her neighbors, especially
the children. By the time I was growing up, many of the trees
Vovó Levinda had planted had been cut off to make room for
the two other houses built in the yard, but my cousins, my sister and I were still able to blow soap bubbles out of papaya-tree
branches and pluck mangos and star fruit out of the trees. That
is, my sister and my cousins would do that; I was too scared to
climb such imposing trees, limiting myself to the much short-

---

[2] Vovô is the term of endearment for *avô* (grandfather); the feminine is
vovó (from *avó*).

er (and thus friendlier) guava and *pitanga* trees, and still crying out for Daddy to come get me out.

Although my grandparents seemed happy with a traditional division of labor, Vovô envisioned a life of paid work for all three of their daughters. When "the little ones" (in Portuguese, *as pequenas*, the way Vovô referred to my mother and aunts till the end of his life, at ninety-three years of age) were born, he suggested they all have names starting with the letter *d* because, at that time in Brazil, workers got paid in alphabetical order; those whose first names began with *a* to *d* were paid first. Vovô expected his daughters to do well in school so they would be guaranteed jobs when they were adults. My mother was not too fond of his rigidity at going over their homework, but she and her sister were working women until retirement age. Whereas my aunts opted for going to work early, Vovô encouraged my mother, the studious one, to go on to college and become a professional at a time when most Brazilian women, regardless of race, were told that their place was in the kitchen.

That is not to say that getting an education was easy for my mother. Vovô was, after all, a custodian, which means that his wages were by no means high. He brought home the books discarded at school, but money to buy books was scarce. My mother told us that, devoid of books, she either had to wait till one of her fellow students had finished with a chapter so she could borrow her book, or go read it at the National Library, in downtown Rio. Because the library did not lend books, however, she had to read them there or copy them down, in longhand, on sheets of paper used to wrap bread, which my mother saved to serve as notebooks. That is probably one of the reasons my mother loves books so much. Determined to spare my sister and me from going without, she would buy books even before we were born so that we would have our own library at home. As a consequence, I grew up being able to do research for most of my school projects right at home and to dream of far-away places by consulting our atlas. I was also surrounded by Brazilian and international literature: my mother gave my sister and me the complete works of Monteiro Lobato for children and those of Hans Christian Andersen. Whereas Monteiro Lobato's children's books were famous, Andersen's were much less known. I read and enjoyed the former, but I really fell in love with the latter. I was fascinated with his world of snow queens and warm beer and of stories that so often did not have a happy ending. As a teenager, I was allowed to read the works of adult writers such as Jorge Amado, Erico Verissimo and, later, Machado de Assis, Balzac, Eça de Queirós and Proust. For poetry, there were the complete works of Fernando Pessoa. In retrospect, it is no wonder that I wrote my first poem at the age of eight (entitled, ominously, "Time Passed and I Did Not See It").

My admiration for my grandfather goes beyond his love of books. I always thought Vovô was such an elegant man who looked great in a suit, tall and with beautiful manners. I also knew, from my mother, that he demanded impeccable table manners from his daughters, at the risk of being banned to the kitchen. When I was about nine years old, I found among our books one entitled *Compêndio de Civilidade* (literally, a primer on civility), with Vovô's name on it. So that was where he had gotten his pointers! I read the etiquette book from cover to cover. It was full of old-fashioned advice, such as the need to send a thank-you note to the hosts who invited you to dinner, leaving cigarettes available in beautiful cases for guests in one's home and how to dress appropriately for different occasions. That showed me, early on, another benefit of books: they can provide all kinds of information, even to those who are excluded from society and denied access to formal education —as children of ex-slaves were in the beginning of the twentieth century. In Brazil, the stereotype of blacks as unfit for polite society, purportedly because we did not how to behave,

was very common in my grandfather's time and, in fact, until
much more recently. It touched me that Vovô would look for
ways to educate himself and his children with whatever was
available. It touched me even more that he would leave those
means for the next generations.

There is one other major way in which Vovô inspired me:
his discipline at working out. Older neighbors tell me that, in
the 1950s, long before it was fashionable to extol the benefits
of exercise for people of all ages, Vovô would gather the neighborhood children and lead them in jogging sessions around
the many trees in his yard. As a little girl, I would sometimes
get up early and exercise with him. He always did so by following a class broadcast on the radio; he took those classes for
over forty years. When he was in his late seventies, he went to
the radio station to introduce himself to the physical education teacher who had conducted the classes for all that time.
He too was an older man, who enjoyed meeting one of his
"students." Many years later, when I was already living in the
United States and Vovô had been dead for two years, I
searched for a gym and realized that I could not afford the
annual fee. The memories of Vovô working out at home to the
radio came back, and they inspired me to look for ways to
work out at home as well. I figured that if he could have done
it through that means, without being able to see the teacher
and the moves, I could do it by following video tapes, which
by then were abundant. For over ten years, I diligently worked
out at home. When people thought it was too difficult, I would
tell them about Vovô.

I have many other sources of inspiration in my family. My
paternal grandmother, Josephina, was widowed at an early age
(my father was only six), which left her to raise her many children on her own. Because of abject poverty, several of Vovó's
children succumbed to diseases. My father tells me he started
working as a little boy because he felt the need to help out. On

the streets of Rio, he shined shoes, he carried groceries to people's homes and he roasted and sold peanuts. At the age of fourteen, Vovó took him to a building in Copacabana, the fancy neighborhood of the famous beach in Rio, and asked the managers to hire him as a doorman. He worked there for several years. Because the job was tedious, he would listen to music to pass the time. A fan of American music, he ended up learning to read and speak English just by listening to the radio. I still have one of his date books, in which he wrote down the lyrics of some of his favorite hits. Many years later, when my father came to visit me in New York, people would ask him where he was from in the United States, given his fluency, and were shocked at hearing that this was his first time in the country; by then, he was in his early sixties. I believe I inherited from him my talent for foreign languages. When people tell me I speak English like a native, I tell them about my father, who, unlike me, did not learn it at school.

Speaking of my language skills, which today allow me to move freely in two different societies, I must once again credit my mother for having decided to enroll my sister and me at *cursos de inglês*, after-school institutions exclusively dedicated to the learning of English. I was aware then that she did that at a significant monetary sacrifice, and I took full advantage of it. By the time I arrived in the United States for graduate work, at the age of twenty-one, I had already won awards as the best student of English, writing and speaking fluently. My ability to speak English without a foreign accent has allowed me to negotiate life in the United States more easily. If the mark of my dark skin has given me an inferior racial status, my "American accent" has opened doors that would have otherwise been closed to me.

In building a context for me to thrive, my parents counted on my aunt, Odete, who was my third parent. While my parents were very dedicated (for instance, my father was the one who told us bedtime stories and helped me with my science projects), they both had to work. It was Tia Odete who stayed with my sister and me throughout the day, getting us ready for school in the morning, feeding us, checking our homework. She could be extremely demanding, but also very loving. When I insisted on going to kindergarten at the age of three because my sister was going, but then cried my eyes out because I missed home, she would walk to school at recess, in the middle of the day, just to wave at me. She would then rush back home, only to return at the end of the afternoon to pick me up. For years, I thought she sat there all day long.

Tia Odete was also the one who took care of our religious education, forcing my sister and me to go to Sunday mass after our First Communion. As a teenager, I had no interest in waking up early on Sundays and going to church long before mass was to start, for Tia Odete was fond of repeating that "mass is to be waited for at church"—that was actually a metaphor for any appointments. To this day, she is always early. Since she took us everywhere, we had no choice but to sit and wait for the doctors, the dentist, the bus, you name it. Perhaps as a rebellion, once she left our home when I entered college at the age of seventeen, proclaiming that her mission had been accomplished and she would go live her own life, my sister and I started being late for every appointment. I, for one, couldn't even tell time, for she had always been my watch. It wasn't until I had lived in the United States for some years that I reacquired the habit of being on time. Now that I'm living in Brazil again, I'm often surprised at the ease with which people turn up even as much as one hour late for a meeting (or don't even show up) without blinking an eye.

Ironically, today I enjoy going to church. I remain weary of waking up early to do so, but I appreciate the spiritual connection and the sheer beauty of the whole ritual, including the architecture and the images. In any event, I recognize that without Tia Odete in our lives, our upbringing would have been a lot more difficult.

My focus on such particular moments might give the impression that what has happened in my family history is unique to me. That is not my intention, however. My family history, I am sure, is an illustration of countless stories of descendents of displaced Africans in the Americas who have managed not only to survive, but also to carve out a life in which there is room for dignity, happiness and fulfillment, despite societal resistance in the form of racial injustice, exclusion and inequality. I have no doubt that everywhere in the diaspora there are a number of stories like mine. After all, to be a descendent of African slaves in the Americas is, above all, to be strong and motivated; resisting the inhospitable conditions of the Middle Passage and then making a life where one and one's children have been regarded as less than human are no small feats. What makes my condition different from those of innumerable Afro-Latinos and African Americans is the space I have earned for self-reflection and the privilege that that exercise denotes. The space and the privilege come from my status as a scholar. I have accomplished this as a result of all of the efforts of those who have come before me but have not been able to speak out; speaking about that now is, then, a type of activism.

Achievements

As a child, when I was asked what I would like to be when I grew up, I would always say a scientist, an English teacher and a writer. I am a social scientist, I have been trained as and have worked as an English teacher, and I write.

How I decided to become a social scientist had a lot to do with television. As is common for the majority of Brazilians since the 1970s, I grew up watching *Fantástico*, a Sunday TV show. When I was about fourteen, a piece caught my attention:

an interview with Gilberto Freyre and Darcy Ribeiro about the miscegenation that characterizes Brazil. For those less familiar with Brazilian social sciences, Gilberto Freyre is the articulator and main divulger of the myth of Brazil as a racial democracy; Darcy Ribeiro was an internationally known anthropologist who studied Brazilian Indians and the Brazilian national character. Although my family had always discussed racism in Brazil openly, I was not aware that there was a science that specifically studied race relations. Up until then, influenced by the *Little Scientist* book collection that my father had given us, I had been fascinated by physics and thought I would follow that path. After having watched the program, during which Freyre declared that "in fifty years, we would be a country of mulattos," I decided to become an anthropologist myself.

In the penultimate year of my college education, I enrolled in Encyclopaedia Britannica's first national contest of scholarships for study abroad. That was fortuitous; years earlier, when I was about ten, my mother had instilled in me the desire to go to graduate school abroad, only we as a family could not afford such flight. The contest required an original manuscript based on the contestants' own research. Interested in the intersection between race and ethnicity, I wrote about a black Catholic fraternity, based on fieldwork and interviews. My choice of the Irmandade de Santo Elesbão e Santa Ifigênia, located in downtown Rio, came about because months before I had heard a member make an intriguing comment: he called himself "African" and a member of that fraternity because it had been founded by Africans. My study then looked at how current members sought an ethnic identity in a country that undifferentiated blacks according to race. With my manuscript, I won one of the ten scholarships, which allowed me to go to graduate school in New York City after having graduated college with honors.

Living in the United States has had its highs and lows. It has been extremely rewarding to fulfill a childhood dream, to have the experience of living in another country. On the one hand, as I have mentioned, my language fluency made the process of adaptation much easier. On the other hand, much to my surprise, in New York I was among even fewer blacks than I had been in Rio. Perhaps naively, because of my readings about the civil rights movement and its gains, I had thought I would find many African Americans at the university, but that was not the case. I also noticed that even intellectuals were often ignorant about Brazilians, so that I was seen either as a person from the "Third World" or as a South American. With that came all sorts of stereotypical attitudes, such as surprise at the fact that I do not have "lots of brothers and sisters," that I could write articulately or that I had read the social science classics as an undergraduate. It shocked me that educated people assumed that we Brazilians spoke Spanish and that they knew nothing about us beyond Carmen Miranda and *Black Orpheus*. On an aesthetic level, it also surprised me that afros and other types of natural hair styles had again become unfashionable, with many blacks opting for hair straighteners (which were called, ironically, "relaxers") and that 1980s concoction, the "Jerry curl." It was clear that the African American identity was in flux and that the United States was trying to insert into its fold the many foreigners it received—not necessarily in the best way possible.

I immersed myself in U.S. life. For both my master's and my doctoral degrees I studied U.S. themes on race and ethnicity. My master's thesis in anthropology dealt with the process of change of Israel's symbolic meaning for the Anti-Defamation League of B'nai B'rith; my doctoral dissertation in Sociology was based on the life histories of forty-five African American fathers, focusing on their parenting and domestic participation. In it I defied the stereotype of black men as incapable of being dedicated fathers and spouses, then much in vogue in the United States and, at the very least, suspect to me given my observations of black fathers in general and my own interactions with my father, grandfather and godfather, the latter who often cooked delicious meals, cleaned and was very attentive toward all of us children. In other words, my life as a black Brazilian informed my choice of study by keeping me attuned to the fact that the way societies view us blacks is not necessary the way we are.

Throughout the years I have lived in the United States, I have always returned to Brazil. The longest I stayed away was in the first two years when I moved north. When I returned to Brazil for a visit, in the mid-1980s, it was going through the transition from a military dictatorship to a democracy. What was most shocking to me, however, was the level of violence that characterized every major city. It seemed that everyone had a tale of assault and robbery to tell, either as a spectator or as a direct victim. In comparison, New York City was much safer, notwithstanding the fear Cariocas (that is, natives of Rio de Janeiro) had of it because they based their views of that city on older films that depicted the subway system as a dirty and hostile place. I became afraid of being in Rio, of leaving home, of taking public transportation. I was not alone. A few years later, some Rio psychologists equated the fear Cariocas experienced to that of Bosnians, concluding that we were undergoing a kind of civil war.

In part, because of my fear and also because I had built a life in the United States, slowly I distanced myself intellectually from my own home country. I continued to go home often, but I did not keep up with scholarly developments. For all intents and purposes, I had become not an American, but an Americanist.

That would begin to change in 2002. By then, an assistant professor of Sociology at Bloomfield College, in New Jersey, I was invited to participate in a panel at the annual meeting of the Association of Black Sociologists. It was while researching the intersection of race and class in Brazil that I became aware of the great social change that had been taking place there: the denouncement of the myth of racial democracy and the implementation of affirmative action policies. Under the title "Race South of the Equator: Reexamining the Intersection of Color and Class in Brazil," my work was published in 2004.[3]

Since then, I have become more and more engaged in Brazilian intellectual life, reading, publishing and speaking about affirmative action. While I have felt the pull of my roots, I have also been able to be both a Brazilianist and an Americanist. Because Brazil often mirrors itself on the United States, comparisons between the two affirmative action programs, be they warranted or not, abound. Therefore, after having spent the summer of 2003 in Rio, I returned to the United States and created a senior course, "The Rise and Fall of Affirmative Action in the United States," in which I examined the history of those policies in the country and also elsewhere, including Brazil. Studying those comparisons has led me to lecture on them both in the United States and in Brazil. I have also had the professional and personal pleasure of becoming a member of the Affirmative Action Studies Network, an international consortium of scholars who study affirmative action policies in different countries. The professional pleasure is obvious; the personal pleasure comes from the opportunity to engage with a number of people from diverse nationalities, who, like me, live bi-national lives.

---

[3] "Race South of the Equator: Reexamining the Intersection of Color and Class in Brazil," in *Skin Deep: How Race and Complexion Matter in the "Color Blind" Era*. Ed. Cedric Herring, Verna M. Keith and Hayward Derrick Horton. (Urbana and Chicago: U of Illinois P, 2004): 197-223.

My nationality, as well as my academic training when affirmative action was nonexistent in Brazil, allowed me to trace the changes in racial thought. Simultaneously, my many years of life in the United States—first, in a context in which affirmative action policies were widespread and, more recently, in a context in which they are being threatened and diluted by "diversity programs"—have helped me to understand the new Brazilian reality. I thus see myself as positioned to analyze the new Brazilian social reality both as a "native" and as an "outsider."

The year 2006 marked the graduation of the first entering class of affirmative action students at a Brazilian university. I was fortunate to be at that very site, the Universidade do Estado do Rio de Janeiro, to witness the event. I was fortunate to have been awarded a sabbatical year; that way, I could both study that social phenomenon and resume living in Brazil amid my family and friends. Professionally and personally, I consider that a major accomplishment. Psychologically, I do not see myself as "the prodigal daughter," nor do I see myself as an expatriate. Rather, I am someone who has managed to live and work in two countries in opposite hemispheres, to maintain my family ties and cultivate friendships.

Meanwhile, I have also become more attuned to the lives of Latinos in the United States. Responding to students' complaints about the dearth of courses on Latinos at Bloomfield College, in 2002 I created "Beyond Black and White: Latinos in the United States," a survey course. In teaching the "course," I learned that Latina identity challenges the traditional racial dichotomy still in vogue in the United States because Latinos may be of any race. I also learned that "Latinos" is a bottom-up term; that is, it was promoted by the people themselves, as opposed to "Hispanic," a term applied from the 1980 census onward to describe several nationalities, which, up to that point, had been counted separately. Furthermore, I learned that, both in their countries of origin and

in the United States, Latinos are subjected to racial hierarchies, so that lighter-skinned Latinos enjoy higher social status than their darker-skinned counterparts. Where does that
leave Afro-Latinos? In the still rigid U.S. racial structure, being
darker-skinned approximates a group to African Americans;
that is, it renders Latina ethnicity invisible, so that it may be
more advantageous for Afro-Latinos to affirm their ethnicity as
Latinos. At the same time, the longer Afro-Latinos stay in the
United States, the more difficult it may be for them to accomplish that due to the still strong hold the dominant group has
in labeling and placing groups in the racial hierarchy. There is
also, let us not forget, the possibility that lighter-skinned Latinos, who look more like the dominant group, will be seen
more in racial terms (that is, like "any other whites") and less
in ethnic terms (that is, like Latinos). In fact, there are already
indications that may be taking place, given the higher levels
of interracial marriage between European Americans and
lighter-skinned Latinos, and a higher level of residential segregation by race among African Americans and darker-
skinned Latinos.

This picture is further complicated when we add the gender dimension. Afro-Latinas must contend with the reality
that, from the point of view of the larger society (be it their
host society or their original one), we are at a double disadvantage: we are black and we are women. That translates into
lower salaries, higher indices of poverty and overall lower
social prestige.

What that all indicates is the possibility that the Afro-
Latina identity is not only an unfinished product, subject to
personal and political negotiation, but also a fragmented one,
involving the obvious issues of race and ethnicity, in addition
to those of nationality and gender. Furthermore, Afro-Latina
identity is malleable, for it must incorporate the features of a
number of diverse cultures that are, for the most part, united by

language, adjust that identity to the increasingly changing nature of race relations in the United States and adapt to the different social contexts within the same society. For example, I would not be surprised to find that Afro-Latina identity plays itself differently in Miami, a city with a heavy Cuban American presence, than it does in areas with a reduced Latina presence.

Looking for Balance

Living both in Brazil and the United States presents another challenge: the differing, perhaps even opposing ways each society views time, work and leisure. Scholars have traced those differences to the colonial past of each society. As a British colony, the United States adopted the Puritan work ethic, much unlike the ways of Brazil, a Portuguese (and Catholic) colony. The Puritan work ethic, still so prevalent in the United States, makes many Americans almost embarrassed to expand their energy on anything but their jobs or accumulating wealth: people organize their lives around work, ask each other what they do as a conversation starter and measure each other's worth by their occupation. To be worthwhile, an activity has to be related to work. For example, exercising is called "working out," thus losing some of its playfulness; it is something one must do to maintain excellent health and achieve an ageless body, but, with so many expectations, it is seen less as fun and more as a chore. Meanwhile, the United States has the highest rates of obesity and all its associated diseases in the world. It is also the country with the fewest numbers of vacation days per year in the so-called developed world.

In contrast, in Brazil work is not necessarily a positive activity. Perhaps because it was the country with the largest number of slaves and with the longest period of slavery, work was seen as something only the underprivileged do. The privilege of having a maid, of hiring someone to do one's work was sought by many, not always successfully. As a consequence, work is something that needs to be done, but not necessarily enjoyed. Let us also not forget the practice of taking an afternoon nap (*sesta*, in Portuguese), which is still done, whenever possible, in Mediterranean Europe, in Brazil and in other Latin countries.

Yet, that is not to say that Brazilians avoid work. One only needs to see the numbers of people who hold more than one job, who complement their income with informal activities, to realize that is not so. In fact, years ago I noticed that, on average, Brazilians seemed to work longer hours than Americans (the Brazilian working day starts at 7 or 8 a.m. for most), only they do not emphasize it. Instead, they focus on family relations and enjoying life with their friends, and they organize their lives around those activities; work is more of a means than an end in itself. For instance, on Friday evenings in Rio, people congregate in bars and bistros downtown as they leave work and spend time eating, drinking and listening to music. I believe that may be common throughout Latin America.

The realization that U.S. society pushes people toward focusing most of their energies around work has alerted me to search for balance by refusing to let work take over everything else. That way, I also honor my roots. In truth, that is easier to accomplish in Brazil than in the United States, for the obvious reason that the surrounding culture, in the form of customs, attitudes and expectations, acknowledges the existence of something other than work. Having been back in Brazil for six months now, I catch myself in full wonder of the many ways people celebrate life, despite the huge barriers of urban violence, major economic inequality, rampant corruption and impunity. Being back home in Rio, I enjoy the ritual of applauding the sunset at Ipanema Beach and going on endlessly about how amazingly beautiful our city is. I now realize how much I had missed turning back on the street and seeing the ocean and our conical hills all around. I crave the smell of the sea breeze. I appreciate the privilege of once again being able to pluck fruits straight out of the trees and talking to my folks without having to call long distance.

Living in Brazil makes the senses flourish. In the purest sense of the word, we are sensual people. By that, I do not mean the exaggerated, made-for-the-tourists images of scantily clad women gyrating their hips in a frenzy, but the awareness that being in touch with all five senses makes us healthy and whole. Even before I left for the United States, I objected to the hyper-sexualized view of black women (especially the *mulata*, the mixed and thus purportedly more beautiful type) in particular and Brazilian women in general that our country exports. Outside of Brazil, it is a source of annoyance to note that people buy into that image and imagine Brazilian women (especially us Cariocas) as prostitutes dying to satisfy foreign men. This idea constructs us as "hot," in opposition to white and European women, supposedly "cooler" and more rational.

Here I do not mean to reinforce dichotomies, but I do believe that our culture allows for a wider exploration of the senses, not because we are "hotter," but perhaps because of our conceptions of time and work. For instance, leaving time to gather and listen to music or gaze at the sunset, as I have mentioned before, without feeling guilty, together with exercising outdoors year-round, as our climate allows, may make us freer to be in touch with ourselves.

I also take care not to fall into the modern trap of believing that science by itself fulfills spiritual and creative needs. Here, too, I think that the Afro-Latina tradition helps in that it is more open to the idea of a spirituality that is more embedded in everyday life. By that, I do not mean to create a dichotomy, in which Brazil would be more "spiritual" and the United States more "rational." What I mean is that I believe the spiritual and the rational are less compartmentalized in

Brazil than in the United States, and that may have to do with our strong African roots.

A Vision for Afro-Latina Communities

Afro-Latinos are the descendents of those who, through their unpaid labor, built the Americas. Yet, to this day, the contributions of our ancestors are scoffed at, and our very presence in our own societies is threatened by racism and socioeconomic inequality.

My dream for Afro-Latina communities is that they come to live in a world that recognizes their differences without equating those differences to inequality. That would be the meaning of diversity: differentiation on equal footing. It makes no sense, for example, to promote Puerto Rico Day parades and then, for the rest of the year, hold on to the stereotype of Puerto Ricans as loud underachievers. Nor is it fair to celebrate the "colorfulness" of Latinos on the one hand and curtail their entry into institutions of power on the other. When it comes to Afro-Latina women, I pray for the day when we are no longer seen as caricatures of "sensual" and "hot" women and are viewed, instead, as the whole, thinking, worthy and, yes, sensual women that we really are. In sum, my vision for Afro-Latina communities is that they come to be treated with the respect that they deserve in all of the societies in which they exist, that their members be recognized as full-fledged human beings with a rich past, a powerful present and a promising future.

A Jane Doe

ANA IRMA RIVERA LASSÉN

En el barquito de papel del ensayo
todo se veía tan seguro,
al otro lado del mar dibujado
esperaban la tía Altagracia, la esperanza
y todos tus sueños.
Aquel hombre sin mirada
hablaba del pan, la tierra, la libertad,
de aquel paraíso asociado, asegurado,
cálido como tu tierra,
puente hacia más horizontes,
cercadísimo
por sólo seiscientos dólares y un susto
que pasaría rápido como el Canal de la Mona.
El barquito de papel era maravilloso,
navegaba sobre las líneas del plano
como nave de retorno de cien guerras.
Tú fuiste veterana de todas ellas

y zarpaste
acomodando tu hambre
entre los de todas las personas solas
que viajaban juntas, silenciosas.
El barquito de papel siguió seguro
navegando a sus anchas sobre los sueños de quienes
vendrán a encontrarte pronto
en el paraíso cálido, tranquilo,
profundo y salado que divide
el dolor de Quisqueya y el de Borinquen.

Personal

Contemporary

The Whispers of the Ancestors Development of a Black, Proud, Panamanian Voice

YVETTE MODESTIN

"Black Revolutionaries do not drop from the moon. We are created by our conditions."   —Assata Shakur

Alaafia. I look out the window to see the light of the day and to my altar to see the pure light that shines on me. I give thanks to the spirit of my ancestors and to the Orishas for their daily blessings. It is in this moment, this silence, that I kneel and give homage to those who guide me with love. I ask for the light to shine on my family and my community. This space allows me to gain clarity as I share my deepest thoughts. Calling out their names, I gather the strength from everything they have taught me. Naming the Orishas, I capture each road they present. As I step firmly on this earth, I know that I stand with them and for them. For many this is work; for me it is purpose. It is why my ancestors and the Orishas have handed me this road to follow with determination and pride.

MY CHILDHOOD HOME IN THE CITY OF COLÓN, PANAMA was called Rainbow City. In the beginning it was Silver City, named after the West Indian silver men who were working on the Panama Canal. When the men and their families relocated to new homes and painted them in the colors of the rainbow, the name was changed. It was Rainbow City and

123

would remain that way until the year 2000, when it was no longer an American territory.

This was the American way of segregation and separation in the Canal Zone of Panama. Instead of colored and white, it was gold and silver. All of the black West Indian families lived in Rainbow City, Pedro Miguel and Paraíso. Many viewed the families in these areas as privileged without acknowledging the struggle that they faced on a daily basis within the American context and, at times, in the larger Panamanian context. As a child growing up in Rainbow City, I felt little of this oppression. I was convinced that the sun shone brighter on my home. I did not see barriers or hurdles. I never saw my skin color as a stop sign.

To me, Rainbow City was a thing of beauty, not a ghetto, because our community emulated the phrase "It takes a village to raise a child!" Everyone shared the same values and experienced the same struggles. Most of our parents went to school and grew up together, then worked diligently to create a safe environment for us. We shared everything, fought with each other and loved each other to the fullest. We were always reminded that we came from the sacrifices made by men like my grandfather, who worked in slave-like conditions during the construction of the canal. I was lucky to hear the stories directly from my grandfather.

No one best exemplified dreams and resiliency better than my mother, Elicia Juanita Modestin Durant. For many years, she was head nurse for the elders who worked on the Panama Canal because she believed they deserved the best treatment for their sacrifices. My mother never spoke of boundaries to her three children. As I think back, it came as no surprise when we were one of the first families to move into what was considered the white area in the Canal Zone: Margarita. The towns and schools were integrating, which meant, to her, that we deserved everything being offered. She fought for a house usually given to pilots and officers of the Panama Canal Commission.

My mother rose above obstacles. Her acts were not motivated by materialistic wealth but by belief and principle, a truth evident even when she became ill. After chemotherapy treatment, my mother kept her hair short and wore beautiful head wraps like those of an African queen. She died three days after her forty-fifth birthday.

At the age of forty-four, my father took on the responsibility of raising three children. He was present for everything, but there were also my uncles, aunts and grandparents, as well as the larger community of Rainbow City. My Auntie Jeanne, who also raised my father after my grandmother passed away, was very influential in my upbringing. She was a woman committed to family and made herself completely available to my sister, my brother and me. The love I experienced from my family and community created a framework of expectation in my daily life. Every member of the community exhibited professionalism in their careers and were inspiring in the way they lived. In our neighborhood alone lived a head nurse, a Panama Canal security supervisor, a fire sergeant, a police officer, a piano teacher, a school teacher and a doctor. Although we lived in a Canal Zone town and went to separate schools than the white Americans, we did not function under the despair of segregation; we considered ourselves equals to any student.

The parents, teachers and mentors in the community eventually fought for equality in our education system. In the late 1970s, the schools were integrated, but I didn't experience the shock and solitude that I heard about in the United States. The transition was smooth because some of my Rainbow City teachers and friends were already integrated into the white schools. My community remained intact. I was never left alone or without the presence of someone from my own neighborhood. My world carried over into the integrated schools.

Growing up in Panama, I did not experience overt race-related discriminatory practices. I do realize that this was my reality and not that of many others, including my parents. I flourished in my environment because I was free to explore. For example, I was not stopped, discouraged or punished for playing a male-dominated or "white" sport, tennis. On the contrary, my athletic successes in track & field with Coach Henry Jones, helped me gain a sense of self. With this came a feeling of confidence, and commitment to myself. Feelings of self-doubt and insecurity occasionally popped up, but I used them to help me grow. As I reflect on my life, I believe I have lived freely, without restrictions, labels or definitions. I know my dreams have not been shattered. My commitment to my work and community have been reinforced.

For the rest of my life, I would struggle to recapture the sense of connection and community I experienced in Rainbow City.

In late 1980s, I arrived in Boston, Massachusetts, to attend Emmanuel College, with aspirations of becoming a therapist. Moving to the United States was seen by my parent's generation as the next step for their children. Now that I look back, I realize that the decision to leave was not mine. It was part of the Canal Zone West Indian thinking. The expectation was that we would have more opportunities than our parents. Also, things were changing at home. The Torrijos-Carter Treaty turned over the Canal Zone, or American territory, to the Panamanian government in 2000. In the years leading up to this deadline, there was a fear of how the West Indian community would be treated without an American presence in the country. I was not as concerned because I spent a lot of time outside the Canal Zone area and felt comfortable moving around.

At the time, a transition to the United States did not worry me. I thought living among Americans in Panama had given me an advantage to interact and engage with white America; they were my neighbors, my friends, and we challenged each other with respect. I realized, once I was in America, that this wasn't the case. My first year on the college tennis team was a rude awakening. I was winning a match when suddenly the other team's coach stopped play and accused me of cheating; she could not believe I was beating one of her best players. It was not until after the match that I realized what had happened. It took one of my teammates asking me aloud what happened and my not finding the words to explain it to realize that it was because I was black. Adding insult to injury, I was told by a black classmate that tennis is a "white man's sport." In America, a line had been drawn, a line that would take away the things that had always brought me joy.

I did not anticipate the level of negativity that came with being black in America. In the United States, being black meant acting a certain way and being restricted to the general stereotypes placed on the African American community of only living in the ghetto, not having an education or a future. White classmates said I was different and I would ask, different meaning what? Apparently, I was not fully black in their minds, and I was constantly accused of sounding white. What was "sounding white?" What was "being black"? These questions caused me great turmoil during my first years in the United States.

My relationship with my African American classmates was difficult. We struggled to communicate because they did not think we shared a common history. Unlike my experience in Panama, where I moved in spaces with determination that I, too, belonged there, in this country the burden of slavery and segregation placed a wedge between black women that to this day requires added dialogue and awareness of the tension's historical context. Whether between white and black or black and black, the focus is on difference.

I could not turn to my Latina classmates for comfort. For the most part, they did not acknowledge me. Light-skinned Latinas separated themselves from me. "Are you really Latina?" they would ask. I did not understand the question. I would say I was born and raised in Panama. That did not seem enough for them. The response was then, "Oh, I thought you were one of them." I would ask, "One of whom?" "A black person. An African American," they would say. "But I am black," I would say. I found myself speaking Spanish every chance I got. There are times I still do it to validate my position. These experiences created a wall between two halves of myself I never thought were separate, the Afro-descendent and the Latina. To live comfortably in this country, I had to choose.

My connection to the place I came from—where my identity was defined and clear to me—began to disintegrate. I began to wonder why I had come to the United States. Was my childhood experience simply näive and unrealistic? Was this country truly the melting pot I believed it to be? Did the civil rights movement really open the door for black people? To calm my anxiety I hung on to things I thought would define me in the eyes of others, for example, wearing my hair long because that was an image people had of Latinas.

I fell into a depression, drowning in these unanswered questions and not knowing who I was any more. I was in shock most of the time, getting to the point where I only hung out with African Americans and did not share that I was a Latina. I did not go into Latino settings so I wouldn't have to explain myself. I learned that no matter how well I dressed or presented myself, some people would not get past the color of my skin. I learned that speaking well meant you sounded white. This still happens to me today, even in the most progressive settings. I ask, can Afro-Latinas be the bridge between the two worlds we carry so close in our hearts?

My journey in this country began with false images and stifling stereotypes, but in a way they inspired me to get involved. I wanted to rebuild Rainbow City, a world that creates a strong sense of self, knowledge of your history and

visions of strength and inner power. I was not ready for a Latino world that denied its African roots and functioned from a
white mindset in America. I wished to create a freedom to be
multicultural and multilingual.

After leaving Emmanuel College, I was concerned about
how I would fit into the larger society. I knew I wanted to help
people. I sought jobs that allowed me to speak Spanish and
work closely with Latinas, so I could stay connected to the
community. My first job put me in a historically all-white
community near Boston. I was the only black staff member,
but the isolation I felt was dwarfed by the experiences of the
children I worked with. I saw how violence at home had an
impact on their development and ability to function in the
world. I decided to work more closely with families.

At a battered women's shelter, I saw how isolated Latina,
immigrant women are in this country. Without the language
and understanding of the system, they are left helpless. At
times, their fear of deportation supersedes fear of their batter-
ers. For many women, it is difficult to leave their homes and
their personal freedom to enter a setting that dictates everything: when you get up, how to speak to your children, how
and when to clean and so forth. This was all done with safety
in mind: for them, their children and the staff. Yet, their voices and what they truly needed to be safe—a home, clothing,
consistency—were obscured by the system. I wondered, was
this really empowerment? I struggled as a staff member to
implement these rules and wanted a way to work with the
women, but in another setting. I met Latinas struggling
through every moment, not wanting to think about larger
issues. I learned how to sit and see women in myriad shapes
and sizes. Ultimately, I wanted to work in a setting in which
women made their own decisions.

This brought me to a hospital setting. Many of my clients
were immigrants whose needs the system was not set up to deal

with. I found myself doing more court and housing advocacy because of the stigma they experienced as battered women, immigrants and women of color. There was no proper translation or explanation of the available resources. When I entered these settings, before I was able to identify myself as an advocate, the staff also acted negatively toward me with a dismissive and judgmental attitude. Some of it had to do with the color of our skins, but also with the preconceived notions placed on families of color who seek government assistance. This allowed me to better understand my clients' experiences. In the hospital, staff members of color were not supported in bringing their own experiences with racism to the table. They were brushed aside and silenced.

Although I understood my clients' situations on one level, I simply couldn't comprehend the violence and pain these women experienced; but it was in this setting that I saw the common struggle of Latina and African American women. The shame and the stigma they experienced were based on the same societal stereotypes. As I battled the institutionalized racism surrounding me, fighting against the white system's desire to silence me, I saw my clients struggling to break down the same walls.

When I returned to the shelter setting, I was more aware of Latinas' struggles and was savvier in the work. I had formed a better definition of feminism from the perspective of a woman of color—we can be moving with white women as a whole to advocate for the empowerment and rights of women, but at some point, white privilege will allow them to get into spaces to which we are still denied entrance. Women of color move as a whole; success of one must be defined as success for all. The experience was still difficult. I felt forced to be someone I wasn't. I was forced to be less Afrocentric in the eyes of the Latinas who ran away from their African roots, seeing it as a threat and less up front with white women who were quick to label me aggressive. By then, I was strong enough to do better work; I was tired of being broken. I realized many women of color work in similar settings. I reached out to two colleagues, Trina Jackson and Carol Gómez, about responding to our experiences. I was then reading bell hooks's book, *Sisters of the Yam: Black Women and Self-Recovery*. It was an affirmation of black women in defining our own history and voice in a society that continues to minimize us. We hosted a workshop called "The Recovery of Our Souls: Women of Color on Feminism," a powerful experience, moving, rejuvenating and strengthening of our friendships. As bell hooks wrote in *Sisters of the Yam*, "Healing occurs through testimony, through gathering together everything available to you and reconciling" (17).[1]

The training was so invigorating that I decided to expand on the idea and host a conference: "El Encuentro de Afro Latinos in Boston; ¿Y Tu Abuela Dónde Está?" It was an opportunity for us to be heard as Latinas and as blacks—and to be proud of both. At no point did I think this would grow into an ongoing organization, but it was obvious to me later that in planning the conference I had laid the foundation for what would eventually become our non-profit organization: Encuentro Diáspora Afro.

Part of what led me to create the conference was the pain, sadness and anger I felt toward the Latino community. It is this anger that led me to own the term "Afro-Latina," as a response to those Latinos who denied their blackness, and to place the Latin American experience in a historical context. I needed to speak to the racism among Latinos, but also show unity between the African American and Latino communities. When I was planning the conference, I sought out people from both communities for guidance and support. Building

---

[1] hooks, bell. (1993). *Sisters of the Yam: Black Women and Self-Recovery*. Boston: South End P.

from this foundation, I cast a wide net in search of advisors from local government, academia and the women's movement, those who had experience planning conferences of this nature or doing community organization.

In City Councilor Chuck Turner I found an ally who told me what I needed to hear. Giovanna Negretti was a leader in the Latino community who connected me with important allies and funding resources. Ester Shapiro brought the academic component. Judith Lennett and Helen Horigan of Northnode, Inc., became my fiscal sponsors. Judith became our voice of reason. Helen especially had an eye for detail and pulled the program booklet together, but these few people are only the tip of the iceberg. With each phone call or acquaintance, I made more connections, creating a solid foundation upon which the non-profit would eventually be built.

My goal for the conference was to create an open dialogue acknowledging the struggles of Afro-Latinos and making the connections with our African American sisters and brothers. The director of the Gaston Institute at the University of Massachusetts at Boston, Andrés Torres, who had written at length about the issue, was key in creating the questions for the conference. This, in turn, helped me choose appropriate speakers.

The conference addressed seven major questions:

1. Are Afro-Latinos in the United States potential agents for changing the racial discourse in the Americas?
2. What social, economic and political obstacles to mobility plague Afro-Latinos?
3. From what networks of identity and power are we included or excluded?
4. Is there a community leadership helping to define the Afro-Latino experience?

5. Is there a shared community vision in the Latino community regarding related topics?
6. Do the same social justice questions apply to the Afro-Latino/as to African Americans?
7. What are the commonalities, similarities and differences with other groups in the African diaspora?

The conference was a validation that such a conversation was needed in Boston. One participant admitted, "This topic has always been deep in my mind but my family does not talk about it. It feels good to openly talk about race." I was not alone in believing this was a relevant issue Boston needed to address. "El Encuentro de Afro-Latinos" emerged as a response to the silence surrounding the rich and complex existence of the Afro-Latino/a identity in the Americas. Our mission at Encuentro Diáspora Afro continues to be bringing together individuals from across the nation, working within the intellectual, personal and political spheres, embracing their complex and mixed identities, and moving toward an understanding of empowerment. Encuentro Diáspora Afro provides support through education, cultural, musical and spiritual celebrations, and political dialogues.

On the day of the conference, a Panamanian friend handed me a book titled *Nuestros ancestros de las Antillas Francesas* by Francisco Marrero Lobinot. I was shocked to discover that my uncle Sulpice "Tete" Modestin was a contributor of information and many of the pictures. I found the names of my mother, aunts and uncles. What brought me to tears was a full-page picture of my father—a sign that I was doing the right thing and that my ancestors were with me. I knew my passion had become my purpose.

My life was at a crossroads. I felt a higher presence, but could not name it. It was at this time that I had my first divination with Baba Tony Van der Meer, a Yoruba priest who divines for people seeking guidance. The Yoruba practice felt like home for me. It brought me comfort and peace that I could not describe in my own words. It also imparted an energy that kept me moving forward with Encuentro. I began looking at my past to make sense of the present and to realize what I hoped for the future. Later, I received my hand in Ifa, a ceremony involving the ancient icon of the Ifa Orisha Yoruba tradition, a portal to wisdom representing the principle philosophical values of Yoruba tradition.

Divination is about how to navigate the obstacles and opportunities in my life. It's about how to benefit from the wisdom of our ancestral practice in finding a solution. It allows one to regroup. As I grow in my practice, I learn to understand verses for myself. Tony stimulates and guides me in my spiritual practice but also challenges me to stop and think. He encourages me to lead with my Ori, or head. I bring this into my development of Encuentro Diáspora Afro. Every step I take has a spiritual presence or meaning. I work toward "Iwa Pele," or good character. As I change the world, I am changing myself. I am redefining what is said or perceived of me from a spiritual base.

As a growing non-profit organization, Encuentro Diáspora Afro focuses on introducing the city of Boston and surrounding community to the issues affecting Afro-Latinos/as. Our analysis of anti-racism work comes from the People's Institute for Survival and Beyond based in New Orleans. We ask: Who are we and why are we invisible in this society? We educate the community through speakers and we present films such as *Human Rights in Quisqueya* by Steve Coupeau on the treatment of Haitians in the Dominican Republic. We exhibit photographs and writings on Afro-Colombian youth by Ayana Jackson and Marco Villalobos. We support the community by hosting bi-monthly community dialogues, addressing current issues, such as immigration, that are affecting the Afro-Latino/a community.

We create a connection to our roots by celebrating our ancestors with an altar of fresh flowers and a chant and libation at every event. One of our most exciting events was the Celebration of Afro-Latinas in Boston. We honored six inspiring Afro-Latinas, one of whom said, "I have been honored, but never for being all of who I am."

This brings me to an important issue: the lack of identity and self-esteem in our youth of color, especially young women. Currently, in Boston, the largest populations of students are Latinos and African Americans, but there is a lot of tension between them because they are speaking across a divide. Because of this, I think it is important to create a space for youth, with a focus on girls, to come together and share their struggles and strengths. We have developed a Young Women's Leadership Project called H.E.R. (Hermanas Exchanging Roots) to bring them together. The purpose is to unite young women, reconstruct their identities and move toward positive change.

But my journeys for Encuentro Diáspora Afro extend beyond Boston. I have tried to maintain a connection to the larger diaspora by traveling to Latin America. Meeting with the members of the Afrodescendent Movement in Latin America and the Caribbean, and witnessing their work first-hand, has given me energy and perspective. My travels also brought me full circle: in Panama I presented at the Afro–Latin American Research Association. It was the first time my father heard me speak and understood how much this meant to me. My family and friends realized the pain I had experienced living in the United States.

As the Diaspora Regional Coordinator for the Red de Mujeres Afro-Latinoamericanas, Afrocaribeñas y de la Diáspora, I represent our mission in the larger international setting. I am honored not only by the position, but that my peers have placed their confidence in me. I learn and share with all these women—my friends, my sisters—no matter how far we are from each other. When I travel to each country, I learn directly from them what the needs of the communities are, but more importantly I learn how connected we are. One of the most impacting trips was to Chota, Ecuador. As soon as I walked onto Ecuadoran soil, I began to cry, as if the ancestors were speaking directly to me, and I felt their joy and pain. My journey is about giving back to the people who have had such a lasting impact on me. It is about celebrating them and telling their stories.

The founding of the new name, Encuentro Diáspora Afro came after a Red De Mujeres Afro meeting in Nicaragua. Since we had changed the name of the organization, from El Encuentro Voices of Afro-Latinos, it has been growing at a pace that seems so natural to me. This is due to the tireless efforts of our new grant writer and my dear childhood friend, Veena Mayani. Every event has new faces. We are creative in how we teach the community, but we are still committed to how we began. Our atmosphere is intergenerational. We have African Americans and Latinos who are self-identified as Afro-descendents and others who are not. I think this comes from my ability to sit in many different spaces. We welcome all.

The journey has changed me as well. I am not as insistent on people defining themselves quickly or easily as Afro-Latinos. Every one will get there in his or her own time. We just want to be there as a support. This change in attitude has influenced my relationship with the Latino community. My message is the same, but my delivery is different. I am aware that we are all struggling to find our footing in this country. I acknowledge that in seeking identity, we are faced with internal conflict and external conflict from family and friends. I hope we can accept our African history, but I know that we will not all get there at the same time. I now know, with great clarity, that I left Panama but Panama never left me. The part that was still with me was my right to be and move as Yvette Marie Modestin Durant.

In my daily life I seek the higher knowledge and wisdom that is Ifa. In every situation I give my full self. I search for my sanity so that I may walk in this world with less weight in my heart. Encuentro Diáspora Afro is no longer mine. It belongs to all of us. We have patience for those who are still looking. It is a place for celebration for those who have found what they were looking for. The question I seek to answer is how do we mend our broken world? My answer today is by building a community that shares and incorporates all of the values I have been describing. Through my spiritual practice, I address this question. It is at the center of my journey. I welcome and receive what comes to me as a blessing.

We cannot become complacent, as the events surrounding Hurricane Katrina showed us. I reflected on that tragedy at the time and wrote in our blog reflections, "My heart bleeds for the victims of Katrina. This brutal showing reminds me of why I am doing this work and why we must continue. As Alice Walker wrote in *We Are the Ones We Have Been Waiting For: Inner Light in a Time of Darkness*, "Katrina may be the start of massive unraveling of everything we thought was whole" (78).[2]

Although I have found some comfort in the United States, I find peace and clarity when I reflect on my upbringing. This journey has brought me closer to understanding my family's struggle for equality and inclusion in Panama. We now have a Día de la Etnia Negra which we celebrate on May 30. On that day, I join my people in Colón and walk through the streets with the light of our ancestors as we celebrate our history, our presence in Panama. One of my most treasured gifts has been

---

[2] Walker, Alice. (2006). *We Are the Ones We Have Been Waitin For: Inner Light in a Time of Darkness*. New York: New P.

my friendship with my mentor, my friend, Mr. Claral Richards. Mr. Richards is the man that led a long fight to get the law passed. He has now become my point of reference as someone who gives his all for his people in and out of Panama. He has sparked a new fire in me that moves with clarity and love. In cutting my processed hair and wearing it naturally, I have experienced a wonderful sense of freedom. This is an extension of my full acceptance of self. As Assata Shakur said, "My life became an African life, my surroundings took on an African flavor, my spirit took on an African glow" (185).[3] I still have many questions about the terms used to define me and how they divide the black people of the world. I think that asking these questions is healthy and shows the ability to grow. It may seem contradicting to many, but that is the world we live in.

Gaining this clarity has allowed me to see myself in the faces of the women from Belize, Peru, Haiti, Senegal and Nigeria. I now look to Africa as my beginning. I still have many questions about the terms used to define me and how they divide the black people of the world. I think that asking these questions is healthy and shows the ability to grow. It may seem contradictory to many, but that is the world we live in. I have more questions now than I did at the beginning of this journey. I struggle daily with the treatment and disparities faced by black people. I am a black woman first and foremost, but I am disappointed with statements that divide African Americans and Latinos/as and leave Afro-descendents of Latin America out of the dialogue. I seek to find a space that brings us all together, not only through Encuentro Diáspora Afro, but through my spiritual practice as well. This is about black liberation, liberation for all. I use the terms *feminist*, *Africana*, and *womanist* fluidly. They identify me, but at times

---

[3] Shakur, Assata. (1987). *Assata: An Autobiography.* Chicago: Lawrence Hill Books.

one will supersede the others. As Clenora Hudson Weems states, "Women of African descent need to create our own criteria of assessing our realities, both in thought and action, believing in womanhood, family and community. It is defined by the centrality of our own experience" (7-24).[4] I cannot be happy about Afro-Latinos/as moving forward if it means that Afro-descendents as a whole are not.

In closing, I return to Iwa Pele. The ultimate search leads me to the many aspects of good character, but there are three that stand out as particularly meaningful to Afro-descendents of Latin America. *Truth* is the ability to share my hopes and dreams in my own words. *Humility* means to value every person and every interaction. Lastly, it takes *patience* to move in a society that has not been inclusive of our voices and to believe that it will happen. The whispers of my ancestors guide me on this my journey. I move with the love for them to tell their story, speak their truth and seek justice and inclusion for my familia, grounded in my Blackness. *Alaafia*.

---

[4] Hudson-Weems,Clenora. (2004). "Africana Womanism: Entering the New Millenium." In *State of the Race: Creating Our 21st Century; Where Do We Go from Here?* Eds. Jemadari Kamara and Tony van Der Meer. Boston: Diaspora P.

La Encrucijada/The Crossroads Where Roots Grow Again

MARINIEVE ALBA

*"Another world is not only possible, she is on her way. And on a
quiet day, if you really listen, you can hear her breathing."*
                                        —Arundhati Roy, World Social Forum,
                                                    Porto Alegre, Brasil, 2003

*"We do not inherit the Earth from our ancestors, we borrow it
from our children."*   —Native American Proverb

M Y LIFE AS A COMMUNITY ORGANIZER CONSCIOUSLY BEGAN
at the age of eleven. Though my Panamanian father had
spent all of my life as a member of one political organization or another, I did not choose to act consciously until my
environment and personal circumstances changed dramatical-
ly. Leaving my home in the South Bronx—where approximately 28 percent of families and 31 percent of the population
live below the poverty line, according to statistics from the
U.S. Census of 2000—and venturing into the world of an
elite, predominantly white, single-sex school changed the
course of my life in ways that I might never have imagined.
This was my first view into the socioeconomic disparities that
characterized life in the United States. While entering an elite
private school was indisputably a blessing that would secure a
superior education for me, the child of immigrant and second-
generation parents, I later realized how deeply this choice
would effect my later political life.

As a child, I had been told that my parents' relationship failed as a result of my father's "other priorities." I also knew that the tensions that seemed to eclipse all paternal family gatherings were rooted in my father's "reckless" lifestyle. When I was nine, my mother partially explained why my paternal grandfather refused to speak to my father and why, at least partially—she had chosen to create a life independent of him.

Hidden behind a childhood photo of a pig-tailed me curt-sying in the yard of St. Helena's Church, where I'd been bap-tized by my father's best friend and only sister, was a photo-copied newspaper article declaring my father a terrorist, a charge that U.S. courts would later recant. The vintage pho-tocopy rendered him a "threat" for his alleged association with a Puerto Rican independence group. My mother explained that while my father was acquitted, his life as a political activist was largely responsible for his rocky family life.

Later in life, I came to understand that my father's love for his children, his family and his people has always been at the heart of his work as a political activist and a leader within numerous community justice movements. I know that he believes that struggling for a more just world *is* a gift to his family, community and the world. He *knows* that he has bor-rowed the world from his children, grandchildren and all those who come after him. Though my grandfather might not have admitted it while still alive, my father's work as a champion of justice must have been inherited from his maternal grandfa-ther, another militant activist during a civil war in another time and place.

The primary lesson I have gleaned, twenty-one years after my mother accidentally showed me that picture, is the impor-tance of family and self-care in any struggle for justice. What I have inherited from my father is a generous heart, a healthy dose of defiance and a deep-rooted disdain for injustice and the dehumanization of my, and all, people. However, my father's sacrifices and recurrent struggle for balance in his personal life, as he struggles for the well-being of others, has taught me to love and nurture myself first so that I may in turn do the same for others. Personal development and self-care are revolutionary.

Self-care—or perhaps self-preservation—is actually where my life as an activist begins. Upon entering the seventh grade at The Spence School, an elite prep school, I quickly learned how different my experience as a working-class Puerto Rican/Panamanian was from those of most other students at the school. Up until that point, I had not yet learned what a Latina was, nor had I learned that we African Americans, Latinos[1] and what are called people of color in the United States were different from whites.

Other than the ethnic whites—namely Italian, Albanian and Russian immigrants in the Bronx—whom I had encountered up until that point, even the concept of "white" seemed foreign. I "knew" that Albanians hated African Americans and Puerto Ricans, and usually attacked us as outsiders in their neighborhoods. I "knew" that Italians called some of us *moulis*, an Italian term derived from the word for eggplant, originally used to designate Sicilians and other "dark" people. I "knew" that Russians were the only "white folks" who lived in the projects and were really poor. Even with this limited awareness of racial and ethnic difference and conflict, it still hadn't quite dawned on me that whites in the United States held power while "we" (the evidently non-whites) did not. Up until this point, my family's consciousness and my homogenously non-white community had protected me from feelings of otherness. Race had not yet fully entered my consciousness.

---

[1] Up until this point, I was pretty clear about national identity, but I had given very little thought to the "ethnic" and "racial" categories that the outside world used to label me.

My life was immediately politicized when, at the age of eleven, I entered the bright red doors of the Upper East Side prep school, where I would spend the next six years of my life. Immediately, "awareness," "diversity" and "integration" became parts of my daily vocabulary. We were "diverse" and other people should become "aware" so that we could be properly "integrated" into *their*, now our, community.

Special classes were planned to reflect the admission of an abnormally large crop of incoming students of color. "Multicultural" student clubs and affinity groups were formed. Meanwhile, my mother reminded me, "No te creas que porque estudias por allá, eres una de esas blanquitas."[2] Mami, with her fair yellow skin the color of overcooked milk, and auburn ringlets much coarser than my short, wavy hair the color of *azabache*, ebony, insisted on distinguishing me from *las blanquitas*, which didn't make much sense to me. My light olive skin didn't seem much darker than theirs, unless I spent the summer in Puerto Rico with my grandmother. Still young and unclear about who these "other" people were, I reasoned that they were pink while we were a much yellower, maybe even greener, bunch since Latinos were always described as "dark olive."

In my mother's family, Tío Jimmy looked like Mami. Tío Junior looked more Arabic than anything. Titi Miriam and Titi Daisy were typical Puerto Rican *trigueñas*, a color classification that supposedly means "wheat colored" in Puerto Rican Spanish. Titi Nancy had a dark afro, while her fraternal twin, Titi Betty, seemed a drop "whiter." Well, I guess Titi Betty had curly hair and shared the wide-mouthed feature that somehow seemed to remind everyone, like Titi Nancy's afro, that we were simply not white. In any case, I knew I wasn't white even without my mother's urgings.

---

[2] "Don't think you are white just because you study down there."

While many of the faculty and staff at the school made earnest attempts to integrate the young women of color in my class into the fabric of school life, and our increased presence stimulated planning for a more representative school curriculum, it seemed to me that some of the students were less committed to these changes. It was not until I was asked by a fellow student to translate her evening meal from English to Spanish for her Salvadorean nanny, and was asked if my mother was a maid, that I knew that getting a good education would not always be comfortable. While I didn't have the challenge of learning without adequate books, supplies and teachers, part of my education in this new place was actually educating others on speaking Spanish, being Latina and from the Bronx, which according to some, was merely a destitute, foreign land compared to the "city" (the students' common name for Manhattan). French, not Spanish, was the foreign language of the elite class; Spanish was a second-tier foreign language reserved for chatting with nannies and maids, or future careers in the Peace Corps.

These experiences, along with those of my fellow sisters —African American, West Indian and U.S. Latina, for the most part—led to my participation in a student alliance founded by two exiting seniors, of Jamaican and Puerto Rican ancestry, as their senior year project. This organization was a safe haven created for "black and Latina" students. The space provided peer support and an outlet for addressing some of our immediate concerns through events and forums led and designed by our small but unified community. We were a diverse bunch unto ourselves. We were economically rich and poor, from urban ghettoes and calmer suburbs, we were timid and defiant. In many cases, we struggled together to carve out a space of our own, while some of our members simply wished that they could blend in without incident.

The first circle of sisters that I inherited at the age of eleven would become the foundation of activism in my youth. This circle would eventually inspire me to take on environmental and racial justice issues, both within my school and home communities, with my sisters steadily beside me at different points on the journey. Learning to function and thrive in an environment that differed so greatly from my home less than five miles away, taught me how to engage my people while still developing relationships with white allies who might not understand my struggle but who were at least committed to examining their role in supporting it. The importance of political solidarity and operational unity, then, constituted the second series of political lessons I learned in my youth.

In the end, I got the best education I could have from a team of dedicated educators—white and black, straight and queer. Leaving my community, if only for hours each day, allowed me to hone my academic and extracurricular interests while nurturing my own commitment to justice and social transformation. The experience itself—of being discernibly "different," of being "poor" compared to my wealthy classmates and of being a "colored" girl with a thick, curvy Caribbean body in a stick thin, lily-white community of women who struggled openly with eating disorders—was probably the single most eye-opening experience of my life. Without being able to articulate it at that point, I actually learned how race, gender and class intersect to shape our lives, dreams and struggles.

Crossing the border between my largely African American and Puerto Rican home community into a world of primarily white American, elite privilege taught me about the resilience of all oppressed people and the inherent power of a unified front. Crossing that border taught me that "my people" were also Asian and Arab, and that "Latino" was the term the United States gave us to explain away the complexity of who we

really are. I learned to embrace the term because it would connect me to other children of Latin America. I also learned that
the United States would never allow me to be one of *las
blanquitas*—at least not with my accent, round hips and
African sensibilities and spiritual foundations; but, that is
another lesson for a later reflection.

America's most deep-rooted fears manifest themselves in
the diseases that plague its imperial subjects. While Eurocentric, patriarchal, heterosexist and imperialistic paradigms rule
the American government, economy and society, people of
color in the United States struggle with defining themselves
outside of the imposed norms and constructions of power.
Sometimes we are our own worst enemy. I learned *that* in a
community of my very own people.

Inspired by the wealth of information and knowledge I had
acquired, and the circle of sisterhood and struggle that surrounded my time at Spence, I arrived at Wesleyan University
ready for struggle. Wesleyan was another elite, predominantly
white institution. I thought, "I can do this. I will continue to
pursue my education and use it in the service of my people," as
I had been taught. Here, I—and we—would be stronger. The
student population of Wesleyan was approximately 2,800 students at the time, compared to my high school's 536. Two
dozen women of color would become several hundred people
of color and, in my näive little mind, somehow that would literally make a world of difference.

What I hadn't actually factored into my plan for continued empowerment was that these "students of color," as I
learned we were called, weren't all from my neighborhood,
where *gandules* and collard greens might be eaten at the same
table. They weren't all from New York City. Furthermore, I
found that many of the "Latino" students from Latin America
and the Caribbean viewed themselves as different from the
"urban" Latinos whose parents had migrated a generation ear-

lier. Some, in fact, *did* think they were white. Actually, they were. Some of them were simply the direct descendents of Europeans in Latin America: the elites. Others were clearly not, but aspired to be. Even some of my fellow urban-bred, prep school "success stories" sought to distance themselves from the Latino and African American communities because it eased their integration, or assimilation, into places of power.

What struck me as odd was the degree to which my privileged education had actually forced me to reject dominant constructions of power. While I continued to value and benefit from academic preparation, professional development and the types of opportunity that education sometimes produces in the United States, I also knew that these very opportunities were often beyond the reach of my neighbors at home. While I learned rapidly and understood the importance of moving fluidly through diverse communities, I never let go of my humble but strong roots. I understood education, vision and achievement to be key tools for unearthing bits of justice in an unjust world.

Success was shaking the dominant places of power and creating new models for growth, reason, prosperity and achievement. While I was raised in a working-class household, even money couldn't outshine my deep sense of personal freedom and justice. While the charm of my quaint (and temporary) New England home afforded me the space to learn and grow, it also reminded me of why home was so important. In a town listed among the stops of the Underground Railroad, I reconnected to both my African and indigenous ancestors, and relearned what I had sought to suppress.

In the context of elite, white America, I was simply a person of color. In the context of still elite, but a regionally diverse Wesleyan, I was a border crosser with mixed allegiances. Growing up in the South Bronx among Puerto Ricans, Dominicans, English-speaking Caribbeans and African Americans, I took

the concept of "blackness" for granted. Racism and racial tension were primarily ethnic tensions and cultural conflicts
between peoples of the African diaspora who didn't know any
better but who shared the same economic and political displacement. We were often bound by poverty or extremely hard
work, fragile relationships to government and mainstream culture (from which we were often excluded by the economy),
and shared cultural values and/or traits, which we often failed
to celebrate. At Wesleyan, these tensions manifested themselves as petty, but prominent, social divisions.

Despite these challenges, I still found my place among the
children of the African diaspora as I got closer to the religion
handed down to me by my mother and even closer to my own
faith. Having determined early on that I would never allow
anyone to make me "less than" him or her, I sought to arm
myself with as much knowledge as possible. Knowledge about
my history, my family, my faith and my ancestors carried me
through four rigorous, and life-changing, years at Wesleyan.
The closer I got to my proverbial roots, the closer I got to
myself, and the more I found my kin. My friends, Nina, Aliya
and Olú,[3] were like me. Urban people of color with connections to the Yoruba tradition known in Cuba as La Regla Ocha
or La Regla Lukumi, they also shared my experience as students of elite educational institutions in primarily European
environments. Though our lives differed in great detail, simply knowing them made me feel better. At Spence, I had one
friend who was familiar with the tradition. At Wesleyan,
members of my community actually practiced the tradition.

Often drawn to the drum and dance elements of the tradition, my new friends' presence reinvigorated my sense of self
by affirming that African culture was as valid as any other.
While my mother ardently affirmed this, my teenage angst and

---

[3] Their names have been changed to preserve their privacy.

displacement sometimes repelled me from regular practice. At Wesleyan, I was able to find faith on my own terms. In high school, I was propelled forward by the spark of justice. At Wesleyan, justice joined faith.

In addition to pursuing courses of study in cultural anthropology and African American Studies (the only two places I could openly study and discuss the historical roots of my faith), I found community again and a new circle of sisters. Committed to overcoming the barriers to African unity on our campus, my friends and I founded Obini, a collective for women of the African diaspora. Taken from the Yoruba word for woman, Obini brought cultural events to campus that highlighted our connections and encouraged inter-cultural and inter-ethnic dialogue across the diaspora. Obini also helped bring Dr. Marta Moreno Vega to our campus. Nina's mother had provided her with the *Under One Sun* newsletter of the Franklin H. Williams Caribbean Cultural Center/African Diaspora Institute and encouraged us to bring her to campus. Casually perusing the newsletter in Nina's room one evening, I decided to pursue an internship with Dr. Vega at the center the following summer.

This too, would be a milestone, as the center would later become one of my homes away from home, and its women my adopted *tías*, *hermanas* and *compañeras* in struggle. There again, I would find myself in a circle of sisters—warriors, healers, *brujas* and freedom fighters—in whose embrace I would continue to grow. More than ten years after my induction into this circle, I find myself going back to grow, learn, teach and grow again. At the center, my connection to my mother's traditions, my father's vision and my own dreams was forged. It is also where I have helped some of my sisters forge dreams of their own.

Beyond its inspiring institutional mission, the center again provided a space to nurture community, culture and creativity. Similar to the *sociedades* that *doñas* at home joined to meet their financial goals, and the *iles* where the *iyalochas* or *santeras* I'd grown up with and loved helped transform people's lives for the better, the center was an ideological refuge and *palenque* (maroon community) smack in the middle of New York City. During my time as program director there, I continued to meet my ideological and spiritual kin, male and female. In this community, I would strengthen my ties to other sisters whose vision for fundamental, holistic change in our communities and the world would take me back to Africa . . . again.

"Fair" by non-European standards and "dark" by European ones, I actually embody the duality of what have been called *mestizos* or *mulatos*[4] in Latin American racial construction. I am, in fact, the daughter of an indigenous and Catalan father, and a fair-skinned Boricua mother of mixed African and European heritage. Those details aside, I had always been taught to celebrate my African and indigenous heritage. While my skin often betrays my politics—inspiring others to seek the Arab, Hindu, North African, Native American or "mulatto" in me—my consciousness cannot.

I am a daughter of the African diaspora, with her roots firmly planted in Yoruba philosophy, indigenous spirituality and an ideological terrain that demands racial justice, cultural equity and human rights for all people. I was born at the crossroads, a composite of multiple histories, identities and traditions, but I am as much an heir of Africa as any other. In Her embrace, I have found faith, strength, vision and power, like the other *cimarronas* who have inherited her gifts.

The children of Africa have many faces. If we all lived in the sun—that is, the sun-drenched terrains of our ancestors —the daughters and sons of the African diaspora would be all warm shades of chocolate, caramel, coffee bean and toasted

---

[4] *Mulato* is a term that references mules in English; it is casually embraced in the hispanophone Caribbean for its "descriptive" quality.

almond with rich olive, copper and burnt cream hues for good measure. When my skin is sun-kissed from visits home to Puerto Rico or another sun-blessed nation, I definitively fall into the non-white category. When North American winters deprive me of light, I am racially ambiguous or white to some, although white America reminds that I am an "other" who will never sit easily in places of power. Those of my people who are darker—often scarred by the color hierarchy and internalized racism that defines our community—remind me that I am light, have "good hair" and can easily pass for something other than black if I choose.

"Pero tú no eres negra, muchacha. Tú pareces más india que na'. Olvídate, se te ve lo gitano, lo español!"[5]

In a post-911 United States, my racial and ethnic ambiguity is perceived as a threat by some.

"Excuse me, where are you from? Are you mixed? Oh, I thought you were Indian or Arab."

Just after September 11, as I made my way down a familiar trendy street near my graduate school, I heard the words "Sand nigger bitch."[6] Unclear about who the racial slur was directed at, I turned my head to see three young white men, drunk and stumbling ten feet behind me. "Yeah, you bitch. Sand Nigger." That is, daughter, sister or wife of terrorist. Perhaps, terrorist. The new "nigger" in the fabled melting pot is the Arab or the brown person, as we learned from countless acts of racial violence following the September 11th attacks. In my old neighborhood in the South Bronx, Yemeni store owners and Mexican workers, became the new targets of epithets and good old American beat downs. I realized soon enough, though, that

---

[5] "But you aren't black, girl. You seem more Indian than anything. Forget it, you look Gypsy or Spanish."

[6] I first heard that term years before in reference to an upper-class Egyptian student at Wesleyan, who was forced to confront his non-white status in America for the first time.

the new targets were not a substitute for the old racism. Instead, 9/11 added another layer of American hatred which not only poisoned some whites, but often people of color, with fear and disdain for the new target. Trying to unpeel these layers, I was again forced to look at myself in the mirror.

American racism is so deeply rooted that just about anyone who doesn't fit its narrowly defined parameters is forced to confront discrimination, hatred and, minimally, ignorance and intolerance. Latin American racism is so deeply rooted that we often fail to recognize and embrace our own people. Latin America, rather than celebrating the true diversity that colors it, and acknowledging the painful and violent history upon which it is built, attempts to hide the truth by repressing resistance and subjugating the millions of people whose daily struggle is born from it. This projection of internalized racism, oppression and Eurocentrism impedes development and justice, and threatens our humanity.

Traveling in Puerto Rico with my husband for the first time, I was disturbed, though not surprised, by the unwelcoming stares and unwelcome ignorance of the islanders. While I was lauded for my black hair and *india* features popularized by a local TV personality, my husband was continually scrutinized for wearing his hair in a natural style. His strong, brown locks, wide nose and brazen spirit somehow shattered Puerto Rico's vision of what black people should be: subservient, uneducated *and* perpetually permed[7] or *pelao*.[8] Like most countries in the Americas, to varying degrees the Puerto Rican consciousness is tainted by traces of European (in this case, Spanish) colonization and the dual consciousness[9] of colonized people who live under the U.S. empire.

---

[7] By this I mean, literally, having permed or chemically treated hair.
[8] Black men in Puerto Rico typically sport short, close-shaven haircuts.
[9] See Fanon, Frantz. (2008). *Black Skin, White Masks*. NY: Grove P.

Stricken by racism, homophobia, misogyny and a ven-
omous class consciousness, Puerto Ricans—and especially
Afro-Boricuas by extension—suffer considerable grief, pain,
violence and dislocation. In this national crisis is where I find
my life's purpose, as a daughter of the African and Puerto
Rican diasporas. Having traveled throughout Africa, Europe,
Latin America and the Caribbean, I have tasted numerous
varieties of racism, and I have also witnessed and experienced
the privileges of light-skinned people across the globe. As the
U.S.-born daughter of an immigrant and a colonial subject, I
also understand the complexity of racism in all of its manifestations, and the intersections of race, gender, class and sexuality in dominant racial discourse.

Ultimately, the battle is against empire and all of its sick-
nesses. As daughters of the African diaspora, however, some
might say we bear a heavier load, one that is nonetheless tem-
pered by a unique legacy of resilience and resistance, to
oppression in all of its forms. For me, in my U.S. context, this
battle means confronting not only the economic, political and
social dimensions of racism and the global struggle for racial
justice, but also exploring and addressing the psychological,
emotional, physical and spiritual toll on my people.

Because I am a "woman of color"[10] rooted in African traditions in American society, this also means challenging
Western constructs of health, "logic" and "reasoning," legitimacy, success and power. My mother, like my Catalan grandmother, taught me generosity, faith and strength in the face of
all hardship. My father taught me how to be a stronger woman
by always setting boundaries and establishing criteria for
respect with men. My spiritual family has reaffirmed the

---

[10]Unlike the Latin American pejorative, this term is used to promote solidarity and unity across ethnic and cultural lines for non-white women in
   the United States.

importance of collectivity, mutual aid and support, and holistic development, like that offered by the *cabildos* (religious fraternities) and *cofradías* (brotherhoods) of Cuba and other Latin American and Caribbean nations during enslavement.

As agents of change, confronting the incessant plague of violence[11] in our communities, we must seek to develop ourselves wholly first. As whole people, we have the power to build whole communities, villages and nations. Once upon a time, I believed that community organizing, advocacy and political outlets were the sole source of freedom and justice. Today, I understand that those tools are simply that: tools that we can count among many others. Preserving tradition, culture, spirituality, (physical and mental) health and creating outlets for personal expressions of creativity, hope, love, joy, unity, peace and justice, are vital elements of liberation.

As the daughter of pragmatic, working-class parents, I never imagined myself to be an artist. Somewhere in my young, mildly skewed consciousness, I had constructed a mission to change the world, void of self-expression and creativity, void of color. In my mind, creating social change somehow meant protests and organizing exclusively. Song and dance and circles of spirit did not fit into my narrowly defined equation of a new world justice and peace for all people.

Today, I know different. The women in my life taught me to breathe more easily and dream freely. Just as my brothers and male comrades have often encouraged the *machetera* in me, so have my circles of sisters reaffirmed that warriors and wise women must give and receive love, too. *This* is the seed of community, creativity, change and collective resistance.

Resistance is in every breath that we take. It is in the food that we eat, the water we drink, the air that we breathe—air

---

[11]This refers to all forms of violence, including crime, physical violence and, above all, state violence via war, incarceration and apathy to poverty (and its offspring).

that some of us struggle even to have. It is in our laughter and in our tears, in our dreams and even in our fears. The feminine face of resistance is bright and clear. In the maroon woman spaces that I have had the privilege of being part of, I have found circles of power rooted in love, faith, inner strength, struggle and hope. Only in these places of truth, where our collective pain and plagues are healed in the open, can new things bear fruit. It is in these places that our roots grow again and that the ancestors guide us toward a better world for our children, and theirs.

A Life Spirals: Journeys of an Afro-Latina Activist

Evelyne Laurent-Perrault

I BELIEVE THAT LIFE IS A SPIRAL ON WHICH WE TRAVEL AND advance by completing cycles. From the moment we are born, we embark on the journey of life. We turn, create and forget, we learn and make mistakes, and thanks to the spiral shape, life gives us the opportunity to make connections with past episodes as we stumble over and over again into new cycles. My spiral has had zig-zag detours as well, for I have already lived several lives within this current one. Amazingly, I am still trying to make new ones!

My journey starts with an ambivalent, insecure, young Black girl, *morenita/negrita,* who was trying in vain "to fit in." Over time and space, my journey has transformed me into a conscientious, empowered, intellectually curious and spiritually balanced Afro-Latina.

Early Years

I was born and raised in Venezuela by my Haitian parents. Most of our relatives lived in other countries; therefore, our family was very small and tight: my mother, my father and me. As was the case with most immigrants, our friends were mainly Haitians like us. Thanks to them, I began to discover politics at a very young age. Dictatorship, "Papa Doc" Duvalier, and symbols of Haitian patriotism were part of my cosmology, even though these marked my life between the ages of four and eight.

We used to visit our Haitian friends quite often. Delicious food, spices and aromas filled the ambiance of those parties, as did the rhythm of Haitian *meringue* songs. I can still envision how grown-ups and children talked, danced and played together. I remember dancing once with a pair of legs and knees. I must have been so small, for that was all I could see of my partner! Creole was the language for grown-ups, while we children were expected to speak French only. These adults were black elite Haitians in exile. Those were the years when Haiti was planted in my soul; even though I have never lived there, their "Haiti Chérie," as the song says, lives in my heart.

My mother died when I was eight years old, and my father married an Afro-Venezuelan woman. We moved to her home, where she lived with a sister and a niece. Moving to a Venezuelan household added a new rich layer of cultural elements to my life; however, this limited my exposure to Haitian culture. Certainly, there are many similarities between Haitian and Venezuelan cultures, but there are differences as well. For example, although food is based on rice, beans and meat stews in both places, the way they are cooked and the spices that are used are quite different. Although dancing is a major component of socialization and entertainment, while Venezuelans dance mostly *salsa* and Dominican *merengue*, Haitians prefer the soft rhythm of *compa* and Haitian *meringues*.

My stepmother is a very intelligent professional woman. The pharmacy of Venezuela's major children hospital was named after her about ten years ago, due to the outstanding service she provided as its director for more than twenty five years; however, languages are not her forte. From that moment, our Haitian friends spoke Spanish with my parents whenever we visited them. As a result, I was almost never exposed to Haitian Creole anymore. It wasn't until I met my husband much later, while living in Philadelphia, that I came across Creole again.

With this new life, we also moved from a middle-class to an upper-middle-class neighborhood located in the eastern part of Caracas, very close to Avila Mountain, Caracas' main guardian and landmark. Both my father and stepmother have college degrees. This meant that we enjoyed some privileges granted to the upper-middle-class. I attended two private Catholic schools in my neighborhood. The first one, where I completed elementary school, was very small (less than seventy students) and was run by Spanish ex-seminarians. Their methodologies engaged all of the students and encouraged us to take leadership roles in the classes. Middle and high school took place in a much larger, Catholic, not-so-exciting Italian-Venezuelan school. There I was the only black student. The rest of the student body was made up of Italian-Venezuelans and other "regular" Venezuelans from middle- and upper-middle-class backgrounds; they were primarily fair skinned.

Always being the only black person in the group added one more layer of complexity to my adolescence: it was a pendulum-like experience. At times, I felt completely alienated and excluded; other times I felt sort of in the middle, neither fully accepted, nor fully rejected. In other situations, I felt included under what I call "the illusion of inclusion."

In Venezuela, as in the rest of Latin America and Latino communities, being black is seen through the lens of a colonial, racialized past that is loaded with prejudice and exclusion of blackness and for the most part of indigenous peoples as well. According to Harvard professor, Henry Louis Gates, Jr., it is estimated that of all the Africans who made it to the Americas, six percent came to North America while the remaining 94 percent went to Central and South America and the Caribbean. The historical evidence shows that even places such as Mexico had a very large proportion of Africans during the sixteenth and seventeenth centuries.[1] Throughout, colonial Latin America Africans and their descendents and cultures were placed at the bottom of the social hierarchy. Although both men and women were subjected to the very degrading system of slavery, I believe that the burden was heavier on women. Black women's oppression resulted from the intersection of the slavery system and the Castilian patriarchal social structure. Even though slavery was abolished in most Latin American countries by the mid-nineteenth century (with the exception of Puerto Rico [1873], Cuba [1886], and Brazil [1888]), attitudes toward black women today continue to bear the stain of the colonial past.

Colonial attitudes considered black women to have no honor, no chastity; they were considered lustful and sexually promiscuous. Raping black women was a common practice and seldom penalized. In addition, many Latin American colonies passed regulations forbidding black women to wear jewelry and fine clothes, most likely as an additional strategy to break down their self-esteem and resilience.

Latin American miscegenation, *mestizaje*, is in fact the result of centuries of white men raping black women, in particular.[2] Unfortunately, emancipation did not end racism, or the socio-racial hierarchy. Ideologies of whitening and miscegenation, *mestizaje*, became the paradigms intended to create

---

[1] See Bennett, Herman. (2003). *Africans in Colonial Mexico: Absolutism, Christianity, and Afro-Creole Consciousness, 1570-1640.* Bloomington: Indiana UP.

[2] See Jiménez Muñoz, Gladys M. (2005). "Carmen María Colón Pellot: Mujer y Raza en Puerto Rico entre las dos guerras." In *Contrapunto de género y raza en Puerto Rico.* Eds. Alegría Ortega Idsa E. and Palmira Ríos González. San Juan, Puerto Rico: Centro de Investigaciones Sociales, Universidad de Puerto Rico.

an illusion of inclusion and to prevent race-based conscious-ness among people of African descent. In addition, these ide-ologies were expected to erase any attempt to recognize or redeem the contributions of the African Diaspora to Latin American nations. I believe this process alienated Latin American societies from recognizing and celebrating their African heritage. In addition, they did hurt black Latin Amer-icans' communal self-image and self-esteem, leading many to self-rejection and shame.

Growing up black, with this hierarchy and silence, was not easy. Fair-skinned Latin Americans and Latinos still conceptu-alize blacks and black women as ugly, uneducated, unprofes-sional, unsophisticated and overtly sexualized. Blackness con-tinues to be categorized as something that needs "improvement" through "whitening." White supremacist notions, as in other places around the world, ascribes very high value, beauty, intel-ligence and honor to white skin, blue or green eyes, straight hair and hues of blonde hair. One can easily see this on any Latino TV network.

As a teenager searching for self-affirmation in a society based upon this ideology, I found life confusing, painful and hard. On the one hand, I also grew up being taught by my father about black pride, negritude and Haiti's unique place as the first independent black nation of the world; on the other hand, societal messages indicated the opposite, making his teachings hard to internalize. The good hair versus bad hair colonial legacy haunted me.

When I was eight years old, a few weeks after the passing of my mother, my father and I traveled to the United States for three weeks to meet and visit some of my relatives. We first went to my father's family reunion in Philadelphia, Pennsyl-vania. After this reunion we went to California to visit my mother's immediate relatives. It was awesome. I met many of my cousins, uncles and aunties. They were (are) so beautiful, elegant and smart. I loved the way they carried themselves. I remember gazing at two of my aunts for a long time, noting what intelligent, talented, articulate and fabulous-looking women they were.

I come from an accomplished and proud family. My father's generation was the fifth generation to have completed college, with some of my relatives going on to earn advanced degrees, or becoming doctors and published writers. On my mother's side, there had been at least three generations of college-educated folks before me. My stepmother was the first in her family to complete college because her family came from a small town where there were no high schools until the 1970s, making it very difficult to go to college at that time. She was able to do so because her family moved to a larger city, because of her vision, and the support of her family. Today, I know that my family and many other black families defy and challenge the colonial discourse about blackness; they have been my main source of inspiration and the beacon to follow.

During my high school years, classmates and friends often told me that I did not "look like" other Black Venezuelan *negros*. Their argument was "you are a refined young black girl" (*Tú eres una negrita fina*). At times, I thought they said that because speaking French as my first language made my Spanish subtly accented at that point. I also thought that it was because of the socioeconomic status of my family and the neighborhood we lived in. After all, I was the only black in my school. My father was one of the only two black engineers who worked at the National Institute of Sanitary Works, and my stepmother was always the only black woman among her pharmacist colleagues. This certainly made us appear special. I also think my classmates had to come up with an explanation for my presence in their milieu. I did often believe that I was indeed special compared to other blacks in Venezuela, but as soon as I would begin buying into this illusion of inclusion, something would happen. A comment, a joke, a look would remind me that for them I was like any other black person. These incidents were a clear expression of the pervasive social rejection of blackness in Venezuelan society, especially within the college-educated middle class. I did not understand this at the time, nor did I have the language to even articulate it with anyone or myself!

It took a while before I came to realize that *all* black people are special, beautiful and refined. Perhaps some of us have not yet had the opportunity to discover it. We are descendents of the survivors of the African Holocaust. That unto itself makes us very sophisticated and strong, and deserves the utmost respect and consideration. Mental slavery plagues our minds and souls, and makes many of us believe that we are underclass people, but we are not.

Venezuela's, and most of Latin America's convoluted and complexly racialized societies and structures, still allow for all types of contradictions. In that regard, I was able to make sincere and long-lasting friendships. During my high school and college years, I partied, danced and visited friends. I went out bowling, to the movies, to the theater, to have a drink, and did what most urban teenagers and young people do, however, within that circle of high school classmates and friends, my blackness excluded me from being a candidate to date. I guess that the illusory refined black girl, *negrita fina*, argument was not enough for peers to dare to cross the racial line. This situation improved a bit during my college years, but then I was trapped into the whitening discourse and, with some exceptions, I dated mostly foreigners and blonde guys.

Later On

In addition to the teachings of my father's family, there have been several turning points in my life that have shaped who I am. The first experience was losing my mother when I was eight years old. Even though I received a lot of support from my father, having to navigate life without my mother from that young age was hard and made me a very strong person. In addition, the void left by her absence developed in me the desire to assist those who needed help, no matter who or what they were.

The second turning point happened when I obtained a scholarship from what was then the Popular Republic of Poland to attend college there. At that time, in 1979, Poland welcomed about three thousand international students every year, mostly from developing countries. Among these students were about three hundred from sub-Saharan African countries and a similar quantity from Latin America. Very few were women and even fewer were black women. Poland provided full tuition, room and board. In exchange, Poland received from UNESCO about thirty-five dollars per student per month, which was given to the students in local currency (zloty) as a pocket-money stipend. Since the zloty was the local socialist currency, it could only be used in Eastern Europe, and since it was just enough, no one could actually save it or spend it elsewhere. This was a way for socialist countries to earn hard currency during the Cold War era.

In Poland, black women were considered exotic, rarely seen, venerated beauty queens! What a change! For the most part, Polish people admired women of African ancestry very much. After coming from Latin America with its baggage, Polish fascination with my looks felt great. I received my first marriage proposal during my first week in Poland! It came from a young, very tall, blonde, blue-eyed, Polish medical student. He told me he had never seen such a beautiful woman in his life!!!! During my two years there, I was approached on numerous occasions in the street, in restaurants and in train stations by Polish couples who had single sons around my age. They would ask me if I wanted to meet their sons as potential husbands. I received flowers from strangers in the street and in restaurants on a regular basis. It became a rule to have songs dedicated to me in piano bars or in spaces where live music was being performed. It was as if that country was worshiping the same blackness that Venezuela had despised, with the added component that Poland was the epitome of Latin America's racial ideal: a white/blonde majority.

I was young, naïve, and I felt I was in heaven. I felt like an ugly duckling who had turned into a fairy tale princess all of a sudden. My battered teenage self-confidence and self-esteem grew exponentially; and by the time I left Poland (two years later), I could not care less about what Latinos in general had to say about my looks and beauty. I knew I was gorgeous!

Nowadays, I clearly understand that this exoticism is nothing but another permutation of racism combined with sexism, where the "weird" "other" becomes an overtly sensual woman, a desirable commodity and an object that can and should be acquired, hopefully through marriage, to display and to fulfill who knows what kind of fantasies. Its sexism was evident because this wasn't a symmetrical experience for black men. Although many young Polish women were interested in dating black men, I never heard that they were approached by Polish parents offering them their daughters for marriage. On the contrary, black men in Eastern Europe have always been the target of racism and discrimination.

To me, Poland was also much more than this. Living so far from home was a learning experience that no book could ever teach me. In addition, most of the other international students who went to Poland did so because of their experiences as political activists in their places of origin. Among my friends were siblings of members of the Peruvian Shining Path guerrilla movement, activists who had worked at Communist Party chapters and former Sandinista guerrilla fighters. Poland was also where I first met and befriended people from Africa.

I met Panamanians who were involved in the movement, demanding Panama's control over the Panama Canal, and Colombians involved with Afro-Latino musical heritage. I met poets, actors, visual artists and amateur filmmakers from other parts of the world, such as the former Yugoslavia and Algeria.

I was also very fortunate to be in Poland from November 1979 to December 1981. These years became the foundation for all of the changes that took place in Eastern Europe during the following decade. Being present in Poland and witnessing the birth of the Solidarity movement, under the leadership of Lech Walesa, was an informal political school. I was living in a socialist country and I was witnessing its people become very involved in contemporary political shifts. This was a critical historical moment to witness and to learn from. Unfortunately, things in Poland deteriorated when Solidarity was banned in December 1981. Several of us felt very afraid, and most Venezuelan students left in an empty train to East Berlin on December 17, 1981. The Venezuelan embassy there helped us to fly back home. I decided to stay in Venezuela.

Home Again

Before going to Poland, one of my interests was to protect natural habitats, something I believed to be pretty subversive. Sustainable development is the only hope for the conservation of natural habitats. These notions challenge the very core of capitalist, industrial and Western socioeconomic organization. Protecting the environment involves two main actions. The first is to study how ecosystems function in order to establish policies that can protect them. The second is a two-sided coin. One side demands finding sustainable, decent livelihood and income for those who live in closer contact with natural habitats. The other side demands the creation of alternative sources of energy for a more balanced, less pollutant and less consumerist Western world. Sustainable practices require international collaboration and multilateral agreements which, for the most part, challenge the profit-making goal of the global market economy.

With this in mind, I enrolled at the Universidad Central de Venezuela (UCV), where I later obtained my Licenciatura degree in biology.[3] A public university with close to fifty-three thousand students, UCV proved to be a very dynamic learning space (31).[4] During the years I was a student, I witnessed three major strikes in which professors, employees and students led different processes aimed at building a better institution. While in school I helped found Provita, which is today one of the most respected Venezuelan NGOs responsible for promoting the protection of natural habitats and wildlife. These were valuable lessons on activism.

A few months before leaving Venezuela for the United States, something very significant happened. I saw the documentary *Salto en el Atlántico* (A Jump Across the Atlantic Ocean), which presented early research done by Afro-Venezuelan activist Jesús "Chucho" García on the African cultural continuities among Afro-descendent communities in northern Venezuela. Although Mr. García was not present at the screening to discuss the documentary, his work made an impression on me. I was so excited to learn that a Venezuelan was searching for the connections between Venezuela and Africa. Besides my father, I had never met anyone in Venezuela who was interested in Africa and its cultural connections with Latin America. I left that theater in a state of

---

[3] A Licenciatura degree in biology at the UCV requires five years of course work, a year of research and a written dissertation with a formal presentation in front of a committee. Because of these requirements, this degree is closer to a master's degree in the United States.
[4] See Angulo H., Mario, and Gregorio A. Castro. (1900). *La juventud universitaria de los años '80*. Caracas: Universidad Central de Venezuela.

ecstasy, with a strong desire to meet Mr. García. Seven years passed before I finally met him.

Overseas Again

Before I could attend my UCV Licenciatura graduation ceremony, I was invited by the New York Zoological Society to work at its offices located in the Bronx Zoo in New York City. I now know that my African-centered experience of New York City was very limited. With the exception of one African American friend I met at work, I did not meet other people of color. I had Venezuelan friends whom I saw from time to time, but I ended up spending most of the time in "white America." I completely missed the Black, Latino and the Afro-Latino experiences that were available in New York City. I ended up living in a neighborhood located north of Pelham Parkway, close to the Bronx Zoo, where I was the only black person. I rented an efficiency apartment from a very sweet and supportive Irish lady who made sure, the day I moved in, to tell the entire neighborhood (while she held my hand) that I was her tenant and that she expected them to treat me as if I was her daughter. Much later I realized that, by doing so, she was securing my safety.

After being in New York for ten months, there came another major turning point in my life. In February 1991, my employer, the New York Zoological Society, hired me to manage a research station in the Southwest Province of Cameroon, West Africa. Since then my life has never been the same.

Africa was much more than what I had ever envisioned. It was (is) very similar to some parts of Latin America and the Caribbean, and yet very different in many ways as well. Shortly after my arrival, my interests began to shift from natural habitats and wildlife to African people and cultures. I began to recognize the roots of many cultural elements that I thought were Latin American, but that we Latinos fail to acknowledge or claim, such as food, sense of humor, social interactions, body language, festivities, storytelling, religiosity and more. I realized that most Latin Americans experience a very Africanized lifestyle but don't know it. I began to understand how main-stream Latin American ideologies on miscegenation, *mestizaje* and whitening attempted to erase the African elements of our culture and our memory, although they could not. I began to question my entire educational experience, realizing that it had never taught me anything about Africa other than the names of the countries and the geographical features.

I became mesmerized by the African people's cosmology, their beauty and elegance, the amazing kaleidoscope of colors manifested everywhere on the beautiful clothing and jewelry that both men and women wear. I was also shocked to discover a very rich West African music repertoire completely unknown in Latin America. I thought that African music was only of drums and percussion. I could not believe my ears when I first heard Tuareg music, and later classical Kora music. What was more shocking to me was that Africans knew a great deal about Latin music. I became fascinated by West African literature, which reminded me very much of Gabriel García Márquez's work. I was also fascinated by how local traditional political structure has kept many pre-colonial components and, in some places, has continued to be connected to spiritu-ality as well.

At the same time, it was distressing to witness how African and Eurocentric political structures are still colliding. In some areas, traditional chiefs no longer have official political power, but yet official political leaders rely on traditional ones to address the citizenry. I learned about African international social conflicts, including some wars that I had never heard of before. I witnessed situations and problems, typical of devel-oping nations, that made me wonder how come there is no more South-South exchange of information. I thought that

Central America, South America and Africa could benefit enormously from ongoing communication without the filter of the North. My understanding of colonialism grew significantly as I realized that developing nations continue to look at former colonial powers for directions on how to develop, failing to understand that in order for that to happen, former colonial powers would have to return all the wealth that they took from their former colonies. This is clearly not going to happen. I understood better that former colonial powers do not want to see developing nations move forward because colonialism has not fully ceased to exist. I also found it very interesting to compare the little I had seen of Haiti with francophone Africa for two reasons: the overwhelming African cultural retentions present in Haiti today; and the French presence—and corruption of high-level officials—in the political processes and economies of francophone Africa.

I compared francophone countries with Nigeria, which was a British colony. Even though Nigeria's political and economic situations are not stable, Nigeria seems to be far more in control of itself than any of the francophone countries that I visited (Cameroon, Niger, Benin and Mali). On this same note, it was very depressing to visit Spanish-speaking Equatorial Guinea; its infrastructure was literally falling apart. At that time, the country did not even have a university. Young people who wanted to continue their education could only do so through scholarships in Spain or in Nigeria. The radio and TV stations played mostly Spanish programs, and during the time I was there, although I did not watch much TV, I did not see Africans on the screen as much as I did in the other countries. Most people I met there really looked to Spain as their "mother country" and expressed regret regarding independence, since the country was in major political and economical distress.

Africa to me was a very intense place. I found it either intensely beautiful, where beauty was breathtaking and beyond description, or with some intensely horrendous and disgusting elements. Celebrations, masquerades, palaces, mosques, colorful markets, people and festivities formed vivid magnificent scenes before my eyes. Yet, it often felt as if I was experiencing a National Geographic documentary. Social life there had no comparison for me; everywhere I went I was greeted with the warmest welcome. Being in a place where blackness is the norm made me feel great. For the first time, I was in a place for an extended period of time where my blackness was expected, welcomed, supported and affirmed with no need for apologies. Blackness was the norm and this situation helped me to become whole. There are no words that can fully articulate the meaning of this experience. In Africa, there was no need to justify my hair style, my features, my nose, my way of claiming music and my ancestry. I wish that everyone in the African Diaspora could spend a significant amount of time in West Africa, experiencing the rebirth and growth that I did.

However, I can't forget the horror and disgust I experienced when I found out about female circumcision, and the times I had conversations with African men about the subject. I truly believe this is abominable and needs to end, but I also believe change needs to emerge from within. The lack of medical attention that occurs in the rural areas is appalling, especially when it affects children and elders. Throughout the places I visited, the condition of most women was dire, regardless of their socioeconomic status. Eurocentric patriarchy is very strong, and many young girls, especially in the rural areas, are not able to attend formal schools and consequently are, in many cases, economically dependent on men. I learned to be non-judgmental about polygamy, as this marriage system can be an asset for women because it creates a tight network of co-

wives who help each other to raise their children and take care
of everyday life chores and beyond.

I took the opportunity to travel by road and boat, and to
visit several places where I had fabulous experiences. After a
camel ride of three hours, I saw the sunset and sunrise at the
Tal Desert, an outskirt of the Sahara Desert in the Republic of
Niger, located close to the northern shores of Lake Chad. I was
invited by one of the Kano emir's in-laws to visit the three
public chambers at the palace in northern Nigeria. I saw a
breathtaking inauguration of the governor of the Province of
Adamaua in the city of N'Gaundere in northern Cameroon. I
attended the second-day celebration of a Tuareg wedding in
the historical city of Zinder, Niger. I visited the research center of Timbuktu, Mali, and was mesmerized by the beauty of
some Muslim manuscripts on display there. While in Timbuktu, I was entertained every day by a woman griot who visited
the house where I was staying; she and my hostess were both
amazing. Griots are community members who are responsible
for story telling and entertainment among many Sahelian cultures. The tradition is usually passed from one generation to
the next through oral history and narratives. Griots are the
ones permitted in their societies to tell sexually explicit jokes
to larger audiences. I was invited to enter and visit all of the
chambers of the mosque at Djenne, Mali, the largest mud-
brick *banco* construction in West Africa; and I slept under the
most amazing starry night in Dogon country, also in Mali.

I was told several times that I belonged there, that I could
be adopted and taught "my ways." I was welcomed in many
homes and was blessed everywhere I went by the sacred joy of
African women's sisterhood.

Ouidah

Among all of these experiences, perhaps one of the most
powerful in terms of shaping my Afro-Latina awareness was vis-

iting the port of Ouidah, located in the Republic of Benin. Previous studies indicated that most Africans who made it to Haiti
most likely left the continent via Ouidah. Because my family
was from Haiti, I knew I had to go to Ouidah, I knew I had to
make this pilgrimage. I arrived at Ouidah around 8:00 a.m. The
History Museum and most of the city's public spaces were
closed, so I walked around the town until places began to open.
A young boy offered to be my guide, and took me first to the
History Museum. The museum is on a fort built by the Portuguese. During the slave-trade era, this fort was one of the last
places Africans were taken before they embarked on the journey of no return. I walked in the courtyard thinking that, perhaps, someone in my family line had walked those same spaces
not knowing what to expect, and taken by fear, sadness and
humiliation. We tend to avoid thinking of the pain that our
ancestors endured. Hopefully, we will never know that pain;
however, I try to think about it as a tribute to their suffering.

Once I completed the visit to the museum, I walked with
my guide to the beach, which was one of the saddest scenes I
have ever witnessed. For me, the ocean is usually an invitation
to bathe, to play with the water and to relax. Yet, the beach of
Ouidah had a solemn and mournful feeling; there was nothing
fun about it. No one was swimming while I was there, and neither did I feel like bathing. Only a concrete cross stood there
as a monument. This cross bothered me, because the church
was significantly involved with the slave trade. I felt that a
cross was not the appropriate monument for this site. (Since
then, another monument had been built that truly pays homage to the site.) I turned my back to the cross and sat on the
sand for a long period of time, perhaps two or three hours. My
guide went home, had lunch, and came back, amazed to have
found me still sitting on the same spot. It felt as if I could hear
the cries, the pleading of the captives, and sense their pain and
fear, their suffering and anxiety. After all these years the sorrow

was still fresh in the air and the water. The ocean seemed like a pool of tears shed by the ones who were taken, and by those who were left behind. I cried and my tears joined theirs and I felt in full communion with the ancestors. I began to feel a sense of responsibility toward them, to feel as if they expected me to do something to redeem their horrid experiences. I collected some sand from the beach, that I still keep with me, and I left. I knew I could not let the silence continue. Recently, I learned that the majority of Africans who were taken to Saint Domingue came actually from West-Central Africa and not from Dahomey, as previously assumed.[5] Yet, the memory of my experience in Ouidah has not lost its validity, especially because no matter where they were taken, Ouidah was the point of departure for thousands of Africans who were forcibly taken through the Middle Passage to the Americas.

After these experiences, my professional interests began to shift. Rather than working to protect the environment, my main goal now became to educate people about the contributions of Africa and its Diaspora, and the role they played in the construction of Latin American histories and cultures. I realized that as long as Latin America continues venerating Spain as the motherland, without acknowledging the indigenous and African heritages in equal terms, it will never be able to embrace its true self and forge more equitable societies.

My Afro-Latina Activism Is Born

I became an activist because I felt compelled to do something to defy ignorance, to educate and to challenge racism everywhere, but particularly in Latin America and Latino

---

[5] See Heywood, Linda. (2002). *Central Africans and Cultural Transformations in the African Diaspora*. Cambridge-UK: Cambridge UP. 211-226, 243-264, 265-287.

communities. It was not a conscientious decision. I began doing what I sensed needed to be done, but I had no idea that this was to lead me down the activist path.

After two and a half years in Africa, I returned to the United States and moved to Philadelphia, where I have lived ever since. I worked for two years at the American Friends Service Committee (AFSC) on the Latin American Desk (Unit). There I began exploring and learning more about the Afro-Latinos struggle in the Americas. Through this work, I learned about the Garífuna communities in Central America. I also met Sueli Carneiro, a strong Afro-Brazilian warrior, philosopher and activist. I learned about the struggles of the black communities in the Chocó, Colombia, and I met the Afro-Ecuadorian educator, Juan García, who taught me about the black communities in Esmeraldas and the Chota Valley in Ecuador. I also heard about the Movimiento Negro Francisco Congo in Perú. While working at the AFSC. I finally encountered the U.S. African American experience and African American activists from whom I learned so much. Aishah, Mike and Zohara Simmons became my activist mentors, and to this day I never cease to learn from them. Both Mike and Zohara were members of the Student Non-Violent Coordinating Committee (SNCC) in the 1960s, and Aishah, their daughter, is an activist and filmmaker whose work "NO! The Rape Documentary," on behalf of black women and lesbians, has been seen all over the world. In the AFSC, I also met the late super-activist Rosemary Cubas and the staff of the Third World Coalition (TWC), who were the other school of political activism and source of inspiration.

I began to give public presentations about my experiences in West Africa and my awareness of the African elements in Latin American/Latino heritage. In January 1996, I had the honor working as the director of the Julia De Burgos Bookstore at Taller Puertorriqueño, located in Philadelphia. By the second week, black Latinos were coming up to me and sharing painful racist experiences they had endured within the Latino community. I also experienced my share of overtly racist comments and remarks by customers who thought that I did not speak Spanish, or assumed that I was not Latina because in their racialized minds "I did not look Latina." One of the byproducts of colonialism in Latin America and Latino communities is the invisibility of blackness and black people. For most Latinos of fair complexion, we black people might come from all over the world, but not from Latin America. I lost count of how many times I have been told that I don't look Latina! At the same time most African Americans coming to Taller do not know there are black people in Latin America and within the Latino community. I found myself defending and validating my blackness while sustaining my Latino heritage.

In September 1996, Puerto Rican visual artist, educator and activist, Siuko García, invited me to give a talk in Puerto Rico at the Semana de Afirmación Afro-Puertorriqueña (Week of Afro-Puerto Rican Affirmation), which is celebrated every year in September. During this trip, I finally met Jesús Chucho García, the Afro-Venezuelan activist whose documentary I saw in 1989. Participating in this conference, and meeting Chucho, infused me with even more activist energy. Chucho's tenacity and commitment has since then been a source of inspiration and support for my Afro-Latina activism. On that occasion. I also met several other Afro-Latino activists who taught me a lot.

More and more of these types of experiences made me think about the need to create a public opportunity for Afro-Latinos, African Americans, other Latinos and the general public to gather and explore and learn about the African presence in Latino heritage. I thought that we needed an opportunity to challenge racism within our communities and to formulate strategies for forming alliances with the African American community across common cultural issues.

I had in mind an event involving two speakers. Johnny Irizarry, Taller's executive director at the time, fully supported my proposal. Together we shaped this dream into a program. Johnny added another speaker and, with a very modest budget of two hundred dollars and the goodwill of the speakers, we were able to host Thomas Morton (then a Ph.D. student), Hector Bonilla (an educator) and Miriam Jimínez Román (an independent scholar then working at the Schomburg Center in New York). The event took place on February 22, 1997, during Black History Month. An African American/Afro-Latino journalist of Cuban descent took an interest in our event and wrote an article about it that was published on the front page of the *Philadelphia Inquirer* magazine on the Thursday before the event. That publicity generated such interest that we literally ran out of space. About 180 people from the region gathered at Taller half an hour before the scheduled time and stayed throughout the program from 3:30 p.m. until 9:00 p.m. We discovered that there was a thirst for learning about the African presence within the Latino community and the Diaspora; five hundred years of colonialism had not stopped our quest for justice. Johnny Irizarry and our three speakers continue to be a very important source of support and inspiration for what I do.

That first symposium was a general discussion touching on Arturo Schomburg's life, the San Basilio Maroon community in Colombia, Afro-Latino facts and ideas about how Latinos and African Americans can establish solid bridges of connection. After the tremendous success of the program, we decided to choose a theme for each year. During the past thirteen years, the symposium has explored music and spirituality, visual arts, literature, culinary arts, dance and movements, religious and secular festivities, herstories, hip-hop, Schomburg's legacy, the racial construct in the Americas, Afro-Latina activists and more.

In 1999, a week after the third Schomburg symposium, I gave birth to my first daughter and left my position at Taller; however, I remained close to the institution and organized the symposium for the year 2000, as a consultant. Ken Dossar from Temple University organized the symposium for the next two years and took it to a more formal level. Since 2003 the symposium has been organized by a committee led by Taller's executive director, Carmen Febo-San Miguel, and composed of several members of Taller's staff, some Taller board members and volunteers, including myself.

The Schomburg symposium is fourteen years old and continues to this day as the only consistent cultural event in the Delaware Valley that, once a year during Black History Month, invites scholars, students, activists and artists to share with the general public their expertise on the African Diaspora with an emphasis on Latino histories and cultures. The event has opened doors of understanding for many who were unaware of the Afro-Latino reality. In fact. I believe that the usage of the term *Afro-Latino* has increased significantly in the region, thanks to this annual event. I have certainly noted how Latinos, who might not have related to their African ancestry prior to this event, now feel pride, and strive to learn more about this hidden aspect of Latino heritage.

Shortly after the first Schomburg symposium, a few of us felt that we needed additional opportunities to continue the dialogue. A symposium once a year was not going to fill our urge; we needed to heal wounds and learn what others have done in the region to bring to the forefront our Africanness. We began meeting in May 1997. Our first meeting was perhaps the most "Afro-cathartic" experience I have ever had. Twelve of us came from various parts of the Northeast and met for about seven hours to share stories, laugh, cry and create long-lasting diasporic bonds, as we were originally from various corners of the Americas. Our common experiences of oppression, racism and discrimination, even within out families, strengthened our common goal of creating more spaces in which to make African contributions visible. We all experienced a spiritual growth at that meeting. We met more times and soon formed Encuentro, Inc., an initiative aimed at educating the general public about Africa and its Diaspora with an emphasis on Latino communities. We organized several events, dialogues and conferences both in New Jersey and Pennsylvania. Encuentro, Inc. continues to support the Schomburg symposium.

Encuentro, Inc. has participated in several international forums and abroad, and was one of the organizations that formally wrote a letter to the Colombian government petitioning for the liberation of the Afro-Colombian Senator Piedad Córdoba during her kidnap in 1999. The membership of Encuentro, Inc. is made up of very committed and outstanding activists, educators, artists and scholars who are also a source of inspiration to me. Encuentro, Inc. members, including myself, have been interviewed on various TV and radio both in the United States and abroad. On one of these occasions I met Marta Moreno Vega, whose ground-breaking work as an Afro-Latina activist has also been a source of inspiration for me; she has also been a strong ally of Encuentro, Inc. The organization has also been an effective tool for connecting together Afro-Latino activists and scholars across the hemisphere. Lately, we serve mainly as an information service, disseminating information about the Diaspora at large through a listserve. Nevertheless, we remain committed to supporting the annual Arturo Schomburg Symposium. In addition, we give talks and presentations on a regular basis to school teachers, college students and the general public about Africa and its Diaspora. Unfortunately, we have not been able to raise funds to structure and solidify the organization at a higher level. We also have not been able to complete the paperwork to become a 501 (c) 3 organization, mainly because of the busy schedule and long distances that separate most of the members. Taking Encuentro, Inc. to the next level remains a dream.

In 2005 I was invited by the activists and scholars Miriam Jiménez Román, Juan Flores and George Priestly to be a board member of the Afro-Latino Project. This initiative supports and strengthens Afro-Latino programs, activists and scholars in the United States. It encompasses research, documentation and education programs mainly of the Latino experience in the United States. Being a member of this project has helped me find new opportunities for developing Encuentro, Inc.

Empowerment of Afro-Latino(a)s, of the people of the Diaspora at large and of the people of the African continent has become more and more a personal quest. Through this journey, I have realized that I need to acquire more information. After six years of working at the Office of Multicultural Affairs at Haverford College as the Coordinator of Multicultural Programs/Mentor of International Students, I decided to leave my job and all of its great benefits to pursue a dream. I put my income on hold (which has not been easy) and became a doctoral student in the History Department at New York University. My program focuses on the history of the African Diaspora as it relates to Latin America and the Caribbean. I am currently at the end of my second year and have recently passed my qualifying exams. Through my graduate studies, I have gained enough insight and knowledge to become, in addition of a historian and an educator, a better and more accomplished activist.

Although we have great dreams for Encuentro, Inc., a lot of work and time are needed in order to take it to where we want it to be. Life circumstances have slowed down that process. My first daughter was born in 1999, and my second one came almost five years later in 2003. Having to find a balance between professional work, marriage, motherhood, being a family member and activism has been a challenge, to say the least! There have been periods of time when I had to put activism on hold because work was very demanding or just because my daughters or my family were the priority. Every time I receive an invitation to a conference or to any engagement, I need to consult my husband's calendar because my availability for activism depends on his ability to leave work to pick up the girls and to carry on with all of the chores. For this reason and more, my husband, Ronel Perrault, is certainly my strongest ally and supporter. In addition to sharing our home responsibilities, he is my sounding board, the one who first hears my ideas, the one who keeps me going. Without him, it would be impossible to do the Ph.D program, or to even think about being an activist and a mother at the same time. Being an activist also implies that I am often giving presentations and thinking about the struggle of the African Diaspora. For this reason, it is very important to me that my husband is a Haitian who is fully immersed and vested in my work. I thank God, for I am very lucky to have Ronel in my life. My daughters, Stella and Maia, are the greatest reasons for continuing my work; I want them to be empowered Afro-Latinas living in a more equitable world. My family is my other source of support; they also share my dream for social and economic justice for Africa and the Diaspora.

During my years at Haverford I was blessed to be working with Sunni Green-Tolbert, who at that time was an Associate Dean and Director of Multicultural Affairs, and with Prof. Tracey Hucks, both outstanding African American women from whom I learned more that I can describe. In addition, I strongly believe my ancestors are guiding me as I move forward as an Afro-Latina activist, who is becoming an historian. The ancestors are among my spiritual guides; they intercede so I can move ahead. I gather my spiritual balance from them and from the notions of order, justice, peace and love that emanate from the Divine Supreme Being.

I am rejuvenated every time I teach something new to someone, every time I am able to reach out to someone who did not know there are black people in Latin America, every time that a light-skinned Latino realizes that there is racism in the Latino community and wants to work for change. I gain strength every time I meet new Afro-Latino(a) activists, and every time I reconnect with long-time Afro-Latino activists and friends. Their energy replenishes mine. My spirit is nourished by the legacy left by women such as Harriet Tubman, Sojourner Truth, Anna Julia Cooper, for they were pioneer warriors. I am also inspired by the legacy of men, such as Marcus Garvey and Arturo Schomburg.

Afro-Latinas, Our Mission, Our Mandate, Our Community

I think Afro-Latinas have a particular place and responsibility within the struggle for recognition, because we are the ones who can bring to light and address simultaneously patriarchy, oppression, racism and sexism. As a community, we can't move forward as long as our womanhood is under siege and our honor and value are contested by society. I believe, as black feminist theory argues, that the enfranchisement of black women will mean the enfranchisement of everyone who is oppressed, because the black woman has been at the bottom of the social ladder in the Americas and beyond.[6]

My dream for the African Diaspora and for Africa itself is for self-sufficiency, to be able to overcome the legacy of slav-

---

[6] See Terborg-Penn, Rosalyn. (1995). "African Feminism: A Theoretical Approach to the History of Women in the African Diaspora." In *Women in Africa and the African Diaspora,* 2nd ed. Eds. Roslyn Terborg-Penn and Andrea Benton Rushing. NY: St. Martin's P. 23-41.

ery, colonialism and oppression that still haunts us and shapes our perceptions about ourselves, limits our life opportunities and keeps the majority of people of African descent disenfranchised. We must learn to embrace our African heritage. We must find the way to gain political influence to create opportunities to empower black communities everywhere.

I dream of living in a world that respects and values everyone's heritage, a world where black men and, in particular, women are seen as honorable individuals, a world where opportunities are given to all so that each one of us can strive for the full development of our souls and spirituality in freedom and harmony.

Fatal Conquests: Racial Imposition in Puerto Rico[1]

María I. Reinat-Pumarejo

N O ONE KNEW MORE ABOUT THE PROCESS OF CONQUEST OF the Americas than Borinqueña[2] leaders Doña Inés, Luisa, Guayervas, María, Yaboneyto, Catalina, Yayo and Isabel, who had the dubious privilege of being among the first Caribbean women to be conquered by the Spaniards. They were all pawns in a chess-game of men, who arrived in Borinquen hungering for power. Some of these women were married off to Spaniards, who considered these arrangements as a means to easy access to the labor force, given that these women were dignitaries and military chiefs of their respective regions (Sued-Badillo, 1989). Dispensing with any romantic connotation, the term "conquest" came to mean imposition, control, displacement, exclusion and genocide to the natives and their descendents.

---

[1] First written in Spanish under the title "Conquistas que matan: imposición racial en Puerto Rico," published in *Claridad* (weekly newspaper) in March 2-8, 2006. I'm thankful to Luz María Umpierre, Raúl Quiñones-Rosado and Saraivy Orench-Reinat for supporting the translation.

[2] "Borinquen" or "Boriken" is the name of the Island of Puerto Rico given by its indigenous inhabitants; "borinqueña" is the name given to the women from Borinquen (Puerto Rico).

From the very beginnings of the colonization process, it is clear how Spaniards—and indeed, all Europeans who charged into our continent with their ambitions—imposed their culture as superior to that of the natives who inhabited our Americas, and to that of the Africans taken forcefully from their homelands. The concept "marriage of convenience" is one of many examples of cultural imposition. Other examples are the imposition of European religions, languages, traditions, art, music and philosophy. These cultural impositions, together with the prohibition of indigenous or African cultural practices that could have inspired a spirit of rebellion, were ingredients in a perfect recipe to take control of the land, its products and the labor force needed to enrich the colonizers and the empire. In many places throughout our Americas, for example, drums and religious rites, chants and ceremonies were forbidden, since they were considered powerful agents of cultural resistance. One of the major fears of the conquerors was the threat of rebellion by our black ancestors. The beating of a drum was believed to be dangerous, except for the purposes of supervised recreation. A slave's listening to a cowry shell, to discover the divine order of things, was probably terrifying to the master because it superimposed a divine and compassionate authority that immunized and protected the slave's spirit against the master's earthly authority and brutal force.

Prohibiting and stigmatizing the use of drums and cowry shells, among other cultural variants, were essential to the isolation of Africans and their descendents from their sources of communication, both human and divine. For this reason, African rituals were practiced clandestinely, hidden by the frilly petticoats of the Catholic saints, in a syncretism that gave rise to Santería, Voodoo and Candomblé, all of them variants of the Yoruba theology and tradition. The Black Councils or Nation Councils in Cuba are some of the best examples of African cultural resistance, since they preserved almost intact the African religious practices and structures (Bolívar, 1995).

In the Caribbean we have come to appreciate, with the passing of time, how music, dance, religion and other distinctive African cultural markers won over the rhythm of life of the masters and their descendents, and fired-up the daily underpinnings of these societies. Fortunately for us, our Black ancestors were able to creatively redefine for themselves Christianity and many other European impositions, in order to humanize their existence and maintain the ancestral thread needed to carry us into our future.

In the scheme of colonial dominance, culture is perceived as the umbilical cord that provides potential nurturing to the desires for freedom. Depriving our ancestors of cultural nourishment, and convincing them that the dominant culture was superior, was essential to attain the colonizers' objectives. Furthermore, establishing the superior-inferior dichotomy as the natural order, and forcing the subjugated masses to accept their place as inferior beings, were both essential in perpetuating and maximizing domination in the Americas. This dichotomy and the concept of hierarchy formed the bases of racial theory, formalized in the newly invented field of physical anthropology. They justified, much to the benefit of Europeans, the dehumanizing conquest of the continent and the emergent capitalist system.

Instrumental in formalizing a hierarchical race theory was the Swedish father of modern taxonomy, Carl von Linné (Carolus Linneaus), the French naturalist George Louis Leclerc Buffon and the German physician and anthropologist, Johan Friedrich Blumenbach, who set forward their ideas and opinions in the eighteenth century. Linneaus, a revered icon of botany and zoology, divided humans into five very subjective and, actually, humorous categories: *Americanus* (natives) were choleric, straightforward, eager and combative; *Europeus* were sanguine, pale, muscular, swift, clever and inventive; *Asiaticus* were melancholic, inflexible, severe and greedy; *Afer* or *Africanus* were phlegmatic, slow, relaxed and negligent; and *Monstrosus* were beings that deviated from these norms, such as the dwarf of the Alps and such aberrations as the Patagonian Giant and the Monorchid Hottentot (Hottentot with only one testicle). Leclerc Buffon believed that "the white race is the norm . . . It is to that we must look for the real and natural color of man." Buffon claimed that some travelers had found Negro tribes so primitive that they could not count beyond the number three . . . and had "little genius" (Gossett, 1997, 36). Blumenbach recognized that the so-called "varieties of human beings" were arbitrary; however, he emphasized that "it would be found serviceable to the memory to have constituted certain classes into which the men of our planet may be divided" (Montague, 1997, 63).

Physical anthropology placed whites at the top of the racial classification system and our black ancestors at its bottom, based on the prejudices of these so-called "authorities." Europeans not only declared that they were superior, but also legislated that their institutions and culture were the most enlightened and the very essence of excellence and normality. European thought, history, logic, problem-solving methods, ways of learning, notion of time, classification and ordering of disciplines, definition of intellect, hierarchies, sense of order, priorities, concept of progress and cultural expressions were all considered superior. Europeans, thus, created a world to their liking and benefit, which would guarantee their dominance in perpetuity.

Marimba Ani, a renowned scholar of African thought, mentions, in her African-centered critique of European cultural belief and behavior, that culture goes beyond its obvious aspects, such as a group's dress or artifacts. Culture serves to inform human experience, giving a group a sense of collective identification and a sense of direction, creating parameters and establishing cultural limits to change, and influencing the group's political potential (1994).

According to Ani, these functions help determine an oppressed group's capacity for collective survival and self-determination, and the preservation of a "natural order." When a group's culture is suppressed, the group loses its sense of direction, making it vulnerable to that prescribed by the dominant group. Conquered people, without the strength of their own culture, would be unable to liberate themselves. Anything that they were to attempt to do for their benefit, based on the worldview of the oppressor, would only serve to benefit the master. Renowned elder and lesbian poet, Audre Lorde, condenses this thought most succinctly when she concludes: "For the master's tools will never destroy the master's house" (1984, p. 112).

In Puerto Rico, a country more than 500 years of colonial experience and, fortunately, of resistance as well, it is imperative to analyze how cultural imposition has affected the process of self-determination. Our modern conqueror, the United States, requires, perhaps as evidence of our unconditional submission, that our psyche assimilate its dominant white English-speaking worldview. Our way of life is shaken up on a daily basis, depending on the mood of the United States' government and its commercial interests. Our waters, our lands, our government and our will as a nation bend themselves to a sense of progress that sows cement and destroys our future. What we eat, what we hear, our sense of family, our ways of solving problems and even our struggle for freedom are constantly infiltrated by the dominant U.S. culture. We have imported from the United States its methods of organizing, its public policies, its models of social well-being and intervention, its sense of time and its priorities. Even as we attempt to transform ourselves and evolve, we end up using structures that corrupt our traditional ways of life.

Sadly, fragmentation and individualism run rampant, even in progressive social movements, as our higher values are not what create our conflicts nor inform our proposed solutions. Institutions and structures of the United States, which are a reflection of the dominant white culture, result in chaos and a lack of will rather than order. We live within a continual cultural dissonance because we accept customs and values that contradict our Caribbean culture and erode our ability to direct ourselves and, eventually, embrace our political self-determination. Yet, the ongoing process of adjustment to our colonial captivity has allowed us to manage this cultural dissonance, even as our collective identity is eroded and fragmented.

In an article titled "Where Are We Headed?", published on March 17, 1998 in *El Nuevo Día*, Héctor Luis Acevedo hits the nail on the head regarding the role of culture in the process of colonial-racial domination. He explains the possible reasons why a U.S. Senate bill proposing Puerto Rico's annexation to the United States lost Republican support in Washington. Synthesizing the United States thinking on race, Acevedo quotes Rep. Newt Gingrich, then Speaker of the House and main apologist for the "English-Only Movement," as he warned of the dangers of incorporating into the United States a population that was so resistant to the English language:

> The personal problems caused by bilingualism are overshadowed by the ultimate challenge they pose to American society. America can absorb an amazing number of people from an astonishing range of backgrounds if our goal is assimilation. If people are encouraged to resist assimilation, the very fabric of American society will eventually break down. Every generation has two waves of immigrants. One is geographic—we call them "immi-

grants." The other is temporal—we call them "children." A civilization is only one generation deep and can be lost in a very short time. Insisting that each new generation be assimilated is the sine qua non of our survival. The only viable alternative for the American underclass is American civilization. Without English as a common language, there is no such civilization.

Obviously, Gingrich does not address race directly in this quote (this would have been politically costly at the time), but people like him believe that U.S. culture is superior to all other cultures and that Puerto Ricans should assimilate for our own benefit. Following the logic of this quote to its inevitable conclusion (and allowing myself a sense of irony), it is clear that Gingrich, in his role as a contemporary racial constructionist, would suggest that abandoning Spanish and our uncivilized Caribbean culture is a reasonable sacrifice to make. In exchange, he suggests that we are being offered the marvelous virtues of the much superior white culture of the U.S.A. Racial architects understand, however, that if the dream of equality and justice were to be realized, under which every culture is considered equal, the control that the U.S.A. has held so splendidly over our Americas would dissipate.

Although we must recognize the differences between the colonizing Spanish master and the Anglo English master, the issue of cultural imposition in the United States follows the same pattern as that observed in Latin America. The domination and subjugation of indigenous, African, Asian and Latino/a cultures was required to accomplish the so-called "settlement" of the U.S. territory. It was not until the 1970s that Native Americans were allowed to freely express their spirituality. Native Americans, like indigenous people in Latin America, also had to pass through a process of extermination, expulsion, exclusion and assimilation. As in the Caribbean, enslaved

Africans and their descendents were isolated from essential aspects of their culture, such as language, spiritual practices and drumming. Congo Square in New Orleans, a designated area where Africans were allowed to play their drums only once a week, usually on Sundays, remains as a legacy of this most regretful history. Drumming was in fact, a powerful tool that nurtured the slave's desire for freedom. The slaves went through a systematic process of physical and cultural subjugation that forced them to redefine and recreate their ancestral culture using resources that were easily accessible to them in the new environment.

As for European immigrants, whenever a group was incorporated into the white collective of the U.S.A., it had to make the ultimate sacrifice of distancing itself from the culture of their ancestors and assimilating into the dominant culture, which might or might not even resemble the culture of its country of origin. Three of the last groups to have undergone this process of assimilation into the white collective have been the Jews, the Irish and the Italians (Brodkin, 1996; Guglelmo, 2003; Hayden, 2001; Ignatiev, 1995). It is clear, then, that in the United States, not all white people have become "white" at the same time; the term is somewhat fluid and malleable when referring to European ethnic groups. The term "white," contrary to common belief, is not necessarily an adjective describing skin color; rather, it is a political term fully functional to the racial arrangement of the United States, where those called "white" gain power, as a group, and remain at the top of the racial hierarchy (Higginbotham, 1978). The term is ever-evolving and contextual to different race constructs and geographies. For example, you could be considered white in Puerto Rico but not be accepted as such in the United States, or in South Africa.

The changing demographics of Latinos offer a clear example of the ever-evolving nature of the race construct and its imposition. Since 2003, Latinos have become the largest "minority" in the United States (Clemetson, 2003). This was anticipated more than two decades ago, when demographers predicted that Latinos were growing at an incredibly fast pace (Spencer, Projections of the Hispanic Population 1983-2080, 1984, 10). To the dismay of many within the far right, who fear the annihilation of the white race, demographers also predicted that whites were not growing at a comparable level (Spencer, Projections of the Population of the United States, by Age, Sex, and Race: 1983 to 2080, 9). More recent projections have intensified this fear as it is estimated that whites will be outnumbered by People of Color by 2042 (Roberts, 2008). Given the political potential of Latinos, and the fact that the race construct might be shaken if Latinos were to awaken to its power. Considering they could fully internalize a sense of collective identity with others as People of Color in the United States, thus magnifying its power, it becomes a political necessity for status quo forces to neutralize such possibilities. The Census 2000 process provided the framework by which whites in the United States could maintain their position at the top of the racial hierarchy by extending an invitation to some Latinos to join the white collective. Throughout the years, though, when asked to select race, many Latinos have shown resistance, preferring instead to choose "Other" as an escape route to the cultural imposition. How to convince Latinos to answer "correctly" has been critical for the government and related agencies.

Latinos have been masterfully convinced to accept race labels through a complex psychosocial process of engineering that disregarded the particular ways in which they conceive race. Clara Rodríguez relates how just three years before the implementation of Census 2000 ". . . it was decided to place the Hispanic question before the race question in the 2000 census because government research showed that 'Hispanics appear less confused by the race question and do not select 'Other' race category as often' when this is done" (2000). The restructuring of the census proved valuable in 2000, as almost 48 percent of Latinos declared themselves whites (Pinal, 2007). Whether those who accepted this categorization are sufficiently light-skinned to equate themselves to whites in the United States remains questionable. What is important, however, is these results are used as evidence to sustain the claim that whites still maintain a large majority, since the percentage of whites jumps from 69 to 75 percent by adding those Latinos identified, if only on paper, as white. This factor has a major repercussion on the anti-racist movement in the United States, as almost 48 percent of Latinos do not choose to identify with the encompassing term "People of Color." This term, contrary to the undesirable term "persona de color (colored person)" in Puerto Rico, is a functional asset in the racial liberation of the United States; it encompasses individuals who are Black, Latino/a, Native Americans and Asians for the purpose of fighting and resisting the racial scheme extended to all in the United States. When 48 percent of Latinos declared themselves white, they became "lost," theoretically speaking, and the unified political power of "People of Color" becomes in fact neutralized.

The 2000 Census in Puerto Rico was an extension of the process of racial engineering in the United States. The census was conducted with the collaboration and mediation of colonial politicians and institutions in Puerto Rico, without taking into consideration whether the instrument was appropriate to our cultural and political existence. The census was so out of touch with our reality that it even asked what type of heating system we used in our homes, regardless of the fact that the only heating system that we use in our blessed archipelago is the warm and radiant Caribbean sun.

It is understandable, however, that in a colonized country such as ours, it would be relatively easy to impose the U.S. census; after all, it is just one more in a long list of impositions to which we have become accustomed, particularly when such impositions come with the promise of financial support to supplement our own meager resources. The census asked us who we were racially, using labels appropriate to the historical-racial reality of the United States. Our own understanding of race was not documented, researched, nor surveyed. It was assumed that the U.S. racial construct was superior to our own concept of race and racism, that it was, at best, generic, benevolent and transferable to our reality.

The result was that approximately 80 percent of our population declared itself white without any racial blending whatsoever, and only 8 percent identified itself as black (U.S. Census, 2000). These numbers were outrageous to many, but to others in the anti-racist movement, they were hardly a surprise. We had forewarned that, based on our creole form of racism and our long history of colonial impositions, this newest ploy would have atrocious consequences. According to the census, there are proportionately more whites in Puerto Rico than in almost any state in the United States. Although this is a laughable proposition, one could argue that now that our racial purity—that is, our "whiteness"—has been demonstrated, we should be more palatable to U.S. politicians, and the notion of Puerto Rico's admission into the Union more plausible. Dr. Víctor M. Rodríguez confirmed the insidious nature of the political agenda behind Census 2000 in an article published in the weekly newspaper, *Claridad*. In it, he describes Governor Roselló's deceitful agenda for unilaterally bringing about statehood for the Island. Even more tragic is the fact that an inter-agency committee had been laboring for years on the island's particular census needs, but their work and findings were ignored (2000).

Besides the troubling thought that our identity is being legislated secretly in the back rooms of the political parties, these results are alarming, especially if we interpret them as a rejection of our blackness and all the major implications of having an identity of African descent. It is understandable, based on our history of colonialism, that many Puerto Ricans would prefer to label themselves as white. After all, through continuous repetition, we have deeply internalized the alleged superiority of whites and their particular worldview. Our own black culture, thus, is frequently reduced to folkloric expressions or a source of comedic relief.

It is crucial that we take stock of the harm done by this new conquering effort and that we understand it from the perspective of our own struggles for survival and self-determination. We need to immerse ourselves in dialogues and collective processes in order to reach the following goals:

- To define the racial labels in Puerto Rico vis-à-vis those in the United States, understanding the historical background that gives meaning to them.
- To note the historical process of "whitening" of ethnic groups in the United States, the reproduction of these patterns in Puerto Rico and their impact on Puerto Rican identity.
- To develop community-based anti-racism processes to confront Puerto Rican racism as well as that imposed by the U.S. racial model.
- To collectively determine how to respond to the 2010 Census, or any other census, in a manner that affirms our Caribbean cultural identity.
- To develop alliances and organizing efforts to influence the Puerto Rico Planning Board and the processes leading up to the 2010 Census.
- To develop anti-racist alliances in Puerto Rico and internationally.

Ilé, Inc., the anti-racist organization that I have represented since 1992, has taken as its charge the development of a campaign to deal with the challenge presented by the census. Our antiracist organizing strategy in Puerto Rico was born out of a deep concern for our national identity and as a response to the impositions of U.S. race labels. A major step in this evolving, long-term effort began in 2001 with the creation of *África en mi piel, África en mi ser* (Africa on My Skin, Africa in My Being), a two-month leadership development and cultural-racial affirmation process. As the title suggests: *If you don't have Africa on your skin, you have it in your being.* This initiative is an interdisciplinary liberatory approach that utilizes history, culture, psycho-spiritual processes and the arts in nurturing the African soul and spirit of our nation. It is led by a team of women committed to undoing institutional racism and devoted to the restoration and well being of our communities. To date, we have engaged three communities in this process: Carolina, San Juan and Vieques. Components of this process are: Taller de imágenes ancestrales (Workshop on Ancestral Images), in which women re-create the lives of our African ancestors and the *maafa* (holocaust) experience of our ancestors; Rompiendo esquemas raciales (Breaking Racial Paradigms), in which we introduce the history of race and its development in Puerto Rico, the census dilemma for Puerto Ricans and a thorough examination of institutional racism. The women in the workshop also learn about cultural racism, especially as it influences our sense of aesthetics, images of beauty and general worthiness. As the closing event, we engage in an illustrated workshop—*África en mi piel, África en mi ser*—which is a full display of fashion, rhythm, history and culture presented to the participants and general public.

África en mi piel is only one of the various efforts in a larger island-wide organizing campaign aimed at getting a more accurate reflection of Puerto Rico's racial composition in 2010.

As "Africa on My Skin, Africa in My Being" so powerfully suggests, culture is not static. It changes naturally as we evolve. However, it must change to secure the well being of our people, and never dilute or clone us in the image of the United States. Puerto Rico has a beautiful culture, divine gifts and favors, all thanks to the cultural legacy of our ancestors. We are a marvelous blend that must not ignore, reject or negate the profound heritage left to us by our black ancestors. They conferred upon us virtues that remain hidden away in our colonial agony—many virtues that we are only now beginning to recognize. This process of re-cognition requires the development of a healthy self-esteem and image. It also demands from us to conceive the difficult possibility that, even with the best of intentions, we could become the mediators, agents and propagators of the dominant colonial culture. Liberating the racial lens through which we view the world is our best decolonizing methodology and the most appropriate homage to our black ancestors, and to all those who forged our nation.

Works Cited

Ani, M. (1994). *Yurugu: An African-Centered Critique of European Cultural Thought and Behavior*. New Jersey: Africa World P.

Bolívar, N. (1995). "El Legado Africano en Cuba". http://www.bib.uab.es/pub/papers/

Brodkin, K. (1996). *How the Jews Became White Folks and What that Says about Race in America*. New Brunswick: Rutgers UP.

Clemetson, L. (2003) "Hispanic Now Largest Minority, Census Shows." *New York Times* (January 22).

Gossett, T. F. (1997). *Race: The History of an Idea in America*. New York: Oxford UP, 36.

Guglelmo, T. A. (2003). *White on Arrival: Italians, Race, Color, and Power in Chicago, 1890 –1945*. New York: Oxford UP.

Hayden, T. (2001). *Irish on the Inside: In Search of the Soul of Irish America*. London: Verso.

Higginbothan, A. L. (1978). *In the Matter of Color: Race and the American Legal Process: The Colonial Period.* Oxford: Oxford UP.

Ignatiev, N. (1995). *How the Irish Became White.* New York: Routledge.

Linné, C. (1767) *Systema Naturae: System of Nature through the Three Kingdoms of Nature, according to Classes, Orders, Genera and Species, with [Generic] Characters, [Specific] Differences, Synonyms, Places.* Paris: Atque Argentorari; Apud F.G Lev rault, blilbiolam.

Lourde, A. (1984). *Sister Outsider: Essays and Speeches.* New York: Crossing P.

Montagu, A. (1997). *Man's Most Dangerous Myth: The Fallacy of Race.* Walnut Creek, CA: AltaMira P.

Roberts, S. (2008). "In a Generation, Minorities May be the U.S. Majority". *The New York Times.* (August 14.)

Rodríguez, C. E. (2000). *Changing Race: Latinos, the Census, and the History of Ethnicity in the United States.* New York: New York UP.

Rodríguez Domínguez, V. M. (2000) "Censo 2000: Nación, raza y el discurso independentista". *Claridad.* 7 al 13 de enero de 2000, pp. 14 y 31; 14 al 20 de enero de 2000, pp 14 y 31.

Pinal, J., Martin E., Bennetti C., Cresce, A. , Jorge del Pinal (2007). *Overview of Results of New Race and Hispanic Origin Questions in Census 2000. U.S. Census Bureau, Housing and Household Economic Statistics Division.* http://www.census.gov/srd/papers/pdf/rsm2007-05.pdf

Spencer, G. (1984). "Projections of the Hispanic Population 1983-2080." *Bureau of the Census (DOC) Suitland, MD. Bureau of the Census (DOC), Population Division. Current Population Reports; Series P-25 n 952.* Washington DC: Government Printing Office. 10.

Spencer, G., (1984). "Projections of the Population of the United States, by Age, Sex, and Race: 1983 to 2080." *Bureau of the Census (DOC) Suitland, MD. Population Division. Current Population Reports; Series P-25 n 995.* Washington DC: Government Printing Office. 9.

Sued-Badillo, J. (1989). *La mujer indígena y su sociedad.* Editorial Cultural. 57-69.

U.S. Census Bureau. "Profile of General Demographics Characteristics: 2000 (for Puerto Rico)." http://factfinder.census.gov/servlet/QTTable?_bm=y&-geo_id=04000US72&-qr_name=DEC_2000_SF1_U_DP1&-ds_name=DEC_2000_SF1_U

Frente al siglo nuevo

Shirley Campbell

Yo quiero creer
que me tocó vivir los buenos tiempos.
Prefiero creer que este
mi tiempo
es el tiempo de los grandes acontecimientos
y de las mejores cifras.
Es que da la casualidad
de que estoy aquí viva
y sonriéndole a mi siglo
a mi humanidad
a mis tiempos.
Estoy
hoy
frente al siglo nuevo
desnuda y sonriendo . . .
Estos son buenos tiempos
tiempos de luz

de territorios liberados
de hijos pequeños o grandes
hijos que demandan sonrisas.
son épocas de mujeres valientes.
creo que me tocó vivir los mejores tiempos
hoy
aquí
encandilada de atardeceres bonitos
estoy más cerca que ayer
de saborear el dulce aroma
de mis noches en celo
sin remordimientos
hoy
aquí
con mi voz abierta
casi puedo nombrar
la piel de mis hijos
por su nombre
me tocó por voluntad divina
amanecer despierta
en el umbral
del siglo nuevo.

Un mundo sin miedo

SHIRLEY CAMPBELL

Me resisto a creer
en presagios y anuncios del Apocalipsis
me niego a recibir sin resistencia
esas voces que anuncian
señales de muerte
de nuestros tiempos …

No estoy dispuesta a morir
bajo la bandera de estos hermosos sueños
que son justamente
los que quiero vivir
suficientes antepasados reposan
por la defensa de los mismos principios
suficientes ausencias
tengo impresas en el ayer.

Sucede que estamos arribando
a la era de la vida y la verdad
sucede que se acerca
el fin de los finales tristes
y de las guerras perdidas
sucede que tengo una niña en casa
que está decidida
a llegar a grande
y sucede que le prometí
un mundo sin miedo
por eso
me resisto a ser parte
del odio y del terror
y me niego a morir
en la siguiente batalla
me niego a recibir llorando el día nuevo
sucede que en casa tengo
una brillante sonrisa sin dientes
que me ha cambiado la vida
y la muerte
y el libro del Apocalipsis
fue desterrado de mi biblioteca
y las noches de lluvia se convirtieron
no se por qué mágico encanto
en hermosas canciones de cuna.

MEDIUM: A Meditation for Diaspora Daughters

LORELEI WILLIAMS

"THE ANCESTORS BROUGHT YOU HERE FOR A REASON: you had something to give and something to receive." This was how a Cuban mentor summarized my life in Brazil as we overlooked the glittering Bay of All Saints from his balcony. It was almost one year after my initiation to Oxum in the Afro-Brazilian religion Candomblé and three months after the launch of Projeto Mentes e Portas Abertas (Open Minds and Open Doors [POMPA]), a youth program I'd co-founded in Salvador da Bahia.

During that time, and the years that followed in Brazil, my identity changed profoundly. I grew to see myself as a daughter of Bahia, a phrase I humbly echoed when Brazilian friends and colleagues first said so. I came to know this land intimately, from its street children to its high priestesses and elected officials, from its jails to its universities. POMPA has since trained forty-two Afro-Brazilian youth for public service careers, connecting them to jobs in places like the State Legislative Assembly of Bahia, where afro-descendents have traditionally been excluded. I recently celebrated three years as a daughter of Oxum, strong in faith, but separated by an ocean from the spiritual family I grew to love.

From 2001 to 2005, Brazil was at the forefront of my identity. Its rhythms, religion, politics and language became an
integral part of my life and work. Brazil was also a catalyst for
my own development as a medium; it was the place where my
capacities were most fully manifested and where they were
tested to their greatest limits.

When some people think of the word medium, it conjures
images of Whoopi Goldberg channeling Patrick Swayze's spirit to Demi Moore in the movie *Ghost* or Patricia Arquette
solving crimes through dreams in the popular ABC miniseries,
Medium. My understanding of what it means to be a medium
is more nuanced. It is a profound spiritual function, but it is
also political and a deeply personal act. To be a medium means
allowing one's body to be used as a bridge, a conduit between
the spiritual and human worlds. In my experience, it has also
meant being an intermediary between two cultures, two languages and Black freedom movements on two continents.

Over the past three decades, feminist and womanist scholars, like Toni Cade Bambara, June Jordan, Cherríe Moraga,
Audre Lorde, Carole Boyce Davies, Gloria Anzaldúa, Alice
Walker, Leilá Gonzales, Sueli Carneiro and others, have artic-
ulated a theory of intersectionality to explain the unique vantage point, challenges and opportunities that Black women
and women of the Diaspora hold as a result of the convergence
of race, class and gender in their lives—and the bridge function they are often called to fulfill. Other authors have spoken
of an intersectionality informed by language, ethnicity, religion and other facets of identity, but the essence is the same.
The greater number of marginalized identities that intersect
within you, the greater your capacity for insight and for injury.

In the work of Congolese philosopher FuKiau Bunseki,
intersectionality can be seen as a spiritual concept: a connecting point between the material and divine worlds. In his
African Book with No Name, FuKiau explains the Congolese

cosmological symbol of the *dikenga*. It is a cross with arms of equal length that symbolizes the movement of the sun and of the human soul through the four phases of life: conception (*musoni*), birth (*luvemba*), the zenith of life (*tukula*) and death (*kala*). The horizontal line in the cross, known as the "*kalunga* line," divides the spiritual and physical worlds. It is often represented as water. The vertical line is the power line where human and ancestral powers are aligned. At the center, each of these worlds and each of these powers intersect. Standing at this cross is to stand in the center of an eternal life force that provides healing and equilibrium.

I felt the full force of both kinds of intersectionality during my years in Bahia. As a Jamaican-American woman, daughter of Oxum and director of an affirmative action project for Afro-Brazilian youth, my body and my body of work placed me in the middle of a privileged but perilous intersection. I stood not only at the crossroads of race, gender, class, culture, language and nation, but also at a spiritual crossroads. This essay is about my experiences and lessons negotiating that middle ground during the past five years in Brazil. Because Black women of the Americas, "diaspora daughters," often live and work on this same cardinal point, this is not just my story, but our story. I offer it as a representation of our lessons, our resilience and our promise, born and bearing us, at the crossroads.

I. The River's Daughter: A Brazilian Baptism

Enslaved Africans from the Yoruba, Dahomey and Kongo kingdoms, and other ancient African societies, carried their religions across the Middle Passage to the plantations and cities of northeast Brazil. During the eighteenth and nineteenth centuries, these traditions merged, were influenced by Catholicism and Amerindian elements, and became known as *candomblé*. Within the *candomblé* tradition today there are three principle nations: the *Nagô* (rooted in Yoruba culture),

Jejê (Dahomey) and *Angola* (Kongo). Uniting them is a common cosmology which emphasizes the sacred connections between humans, nature and the divine. *Candomblé* practitioners believe that God's (Olodumaré's) power is manifested through various forces of nature, represented by the *orixás*. We worship sixteen principle *orixás*. Among the most popular are Exú (keeper of the crossroads), Ogum (who represents metal, war, strength and technology), Xangô (justice, fire, thunder), Oxum (love, rivers, healing, creativity) and Oxalá (peace and wisdom), among others. Throughout Brazil, conservative government estimates count more than 300,000 *terreiros* or houses of worship. From slavery to the present, *candomblé terreiros* have been a traditional mainstay of Black resistance. *Candomblé*'s food, music, dance and spiritual beliefs form the staples of Brazilian culture and identity. Salvador da Bahia, formerly one of the largest slave ports in the Americas, is known as the birthplace of *candomblé*; it is considered a "Black Rome." It is also the site of my own birth as a daughter of Oxum.

My *terreiro* is descended from one of the first houses of worship in Brazil; it was founded in 1889. It is located in Engenho Velho da Federação, a neighborhood renowned for the high density of *candomblé* houses in the same way that Harlem is known for its historic and abundant churches. In 2000, when I first visited a ceremony there as a tourist, I had no idea of the role this *terreiro* would eventually play in my life:

The red and white striped taxi pulled to a stop in front of a wrought-iron gate. My twin sister and I fumbled with the strangely colored money and paid the driver. Dozens of people moved up and down the main street, some barefoot in halter tops and shorts, others wearing button-down shirts and slacks despite the heat. Down the hills, on either side of the main street, shanties dotted the landscape. Houses piled closely on top of each other were lit like fireflies in the Brazilian night. It was a Saturday night and samba music was blaring from an open-air bar on the corner.

The white stone building, behind the gate, sat in quiet contrast to the street. Colorful banners fluttered like birds in a breeze that blew gently as we opened the gate. My sister and I, in our identical white dresses, followed our tour guide to the building entrance. Inside the large square shaped room, there were already a number of people gathered, including several tourists. The clay floor was covered in a carpet of dark green leaves. Streams of small flags hung from the rafters. In the center of the room, a red stone pillar was surrounded by exquisitely carved wooden thrones that pointed in the cardinal directions. Opposite the door were three drums of varying sizes, dressed with yellow bows.

Eventually, three teenaged boys took their places at the drums and began to play, using their hands and thin wooden sticks. A stately woman, dressed in what looked like a nineteenth century hoop skirt and a white head wrap, sat down in another throne-like chair opposite the center pole, and another woman sat on her left. She held a gilded double bell in her elegant hand. Her head poised and expectant, the priestess looked toward a curtain that was opening across from her.

A long line of brown women began to file out from behind the curtain, dancing solemnly. Each wore variations of embroidered white blouses with pleated cuffs, a piece of intricately patterned cloth wrapped around their upper bodies, and tied in place with a large bow. Their dress was exquisite: intricately rendered patterns on lace, silk and cotton. The women's feet were bare. They filed into a circle around the pole, singing. As they circled, each saluted the priestess and other elders by prostrating themselves on the floor or kissing the elders' hands. Their steps were slow and measured; mostly small variations of a two step, moving with arms at angles to their waists, moving in and out away from their bodies. The movements would vary into complex sequences then return to a simple step. Whenever the drums stopped, the women would also pause, some sat halfway on the ground. Seconds later, as a new song began, the women would salute the earth, some prostrating fully and others reaching their fingertips to the floor, then touching their foreheads.

The women were beautiful varying shades of brown from my mother's light-skinned olive color to my aunt's deep chocolate brown. They ranged greatly in age from an older dark-skinned woman with corn-rowed white hair to a statuesque teenager with a halo of an afro. There was a hypnotic quality to their dance. Although they were so distinct, and their movements personalized, it was as if they moved with one body. The drummers seemed to be only an extension of the drums. The whole room rocked in the steady wave of sound, one boat traveling together toward the heavens, every wave a higher level.

The pace of the drumming began to quicken and the songs changed from a somber tone to one of pure joy. The emotion in their voices reminded me of a gospel choir; it was infectious. The drums became louder, faster, more insistent. Then the orixás came down. I remembered seeing a Masai boy catch the spirit like this in Kenya years ago. I remembered this scene, the sudden quickening of the spirit making human contact, countless other times in my Harlem church. One by one, these women made the transition between human and divine, receiving the power of their orixás into their bodies. Each woman became a dancing altar. Some would bend suddenly at the waist, shoulders trembling, a wave passing through their bodies. One quietly cried as she danced, swaying out of balance, overwhelmed; then, just as quickly, she took on a peaceful and purposeful stride. The worshippers beside me sang louder, shouting names I did not know. One by one, almost all the women in the line caught the spirit.

Attending women that didn't catch the spirit wiped the perspiration from the dancer's faces and attended to them with a palpable love and devotion. When the music stopped, the women were led back through the same curtain they had come through. After a long *pause, the drumming started up again, but this time the women who came through the curtain were unrecognizable.* They wore even more ornate and gorgeous dresses, and carried silver and brass ornaments or flowers in their hands. Many wore veils made of satin and tiny beads that matched the color of their dresses. The tourists in the room, myself included, let out an audible gasp. They were breathtaking.

I noticed that as the orixás danced around the pole this time, the surrounding community put up their hands in the direction of the dancer's bodies. I understood why. As one woman passed, the air around her seemed electrically charged, like a mini thunderstorm. It raised the hairs on my arm and sent a feeling like light through me.

Sometimes the orixás would dance out of the circle to embrace people in the crowd. This embrace, as I watched it, was familiar to me somehow. They hugged slowly and firmly, first on the left and then on the right side. Some of the people in the room were also catching the spirit. Sometimes they would be half-carried behind the curtain and other times, one of the women would drape them in a white cloth until the trembling stopped. The orixás continued the embrace and danced long into the night.

Toward the end of the ceremony, a group of young women began bringing heaping plates of food from another doorway and people began to eat. These foods, I was told, were typical "Bahian" food, each dish consecrated to a specific orixá. While we ate, the drums slowed to a final stop. The women and the orixás returned behind the lace curtain. It was 2000. When I returned home to New York City, I drew everything in my journal from memory. I had never felt or seen anything like this, and yet it felt deeply familiar. I wanted to remember.

In three years time, I would learn the names of these women; they would become my irmãs-do-santo, my god-sisters. The majestic woman that called them from behind the curtain became my mãe-do-santo, my god-mother. That house became my house.

The sacred circle widened to accept me. Oxum opened her arms
and made me her daughter.

You do not choose initiation; it chooses you. But early on
something in you knows. Throughout my adolescence, I was
aware of the protection and presence of spirit, though I did not
have a name for it. My family was not a religious one. I found
my way to church and to the Bible as a teenager, and both
continue to be a mainstay of my faith practice. Along with my
faith, I always felt that something in my spirit was not always
addressed; there was a place that the words of the preacher or
the lyrics of the gospel songs I loved did not attend to. I felt
the urge before I could name it. The first sign came with my
grandmother's visits. She died one month before my twin sister and I were born, but she often visited us, offering her comfort and guidance. On a trip to Louisiana at fifteen, I felt her
with a strength I'd never known, walking through a field of
wildflowers alone, their scent and her presence were in the air
with me. I wrote something down that day. I came to know the
divine was much closer than I had thought. Early visits to
Cuban *bembés* with friends confirmed this. When the spirits
danced, the insistent pull and comfort of the drum felt deeply
familiar. However, I never felt drawn to join one of the many
communities in New York. Some special connection existed
in Brazil, though. In Bahia, all of my spiritual awareness, spiritual fluency and ancestral connections manifested themselves
more powerfully than they ever had in my life.

There are few words to describe the intimacy and the
power of my experiences in *candomblé*; it is not a journey easily transformed into language. Certain details are too sacred to
share; others are simply beyond my linguistic capacity. The
theology of *candomblé* is not captured in any one sacred text,
like a Bible, Torah or Koran. The oral tradition is the primary
vehicle for preserving the teachings of the religion. *Can-*

domblé's most instructive wisdom is inscribed in leaves, shells, drum beats and bodies, in my head, and in the instructive music of my heartbeat. It is an inner knowing that arrives wordless, as wind, as breath.

If I had to articulate the meaning of my experiences in *candomblé*, it would be about the healing power of nature, of the sacred circle (the *roda*) of family, of cellular instruction, of rebirth. I learned that my body is a bridge. I learned that a special combination of dance, drum and prayer can turn you into a living altar. I learned that not all knowledge is passed through the word. I learned that the ancestor's desires have always been our own. I learned that alignment with the *orixás* walking with and in me could give me power to fulfill whatever I dared or dreamed. I learned about flight without ever leaving the ground. I found a place I felt I belonged to before birth and returned to it; a part of my soul came home. I felt a peace that I had not known with such consistency. My life felt aligned, in proper order. In the circle of dance, I understood the importance of diversity in unity. We each brought our individuality to the dance, informed by our *orixá*, but we ultimately danced the same dance within one same circle. Even when I was not in the circle, my place in it remained. This connection to community was profoundly healing. I found myself in the midst of a sacred second family. In the circle, I have a place and a responsibility, as both student and eventually as a teacher. Above all, I have a duty, an *obrigação* to my *orixá*, as a conduit of her energy. It is through this obligation, I am aligned to the spirit of my head, to my higher self and to my destiny.

My path in *candomblé* has held as much challenge as beauty. In the early months as an *abian* (non-initiated novice) having recently arrived from New York, my Portuguese did not allow me to understand the nuances of the little that was explained to me about the various rituals of the house. By definition, you do not ask questions and yet I had always been

educated to question; it is my nature. Even on the days I dared
to ask, I could not always understand the answers. Beyond language difficulty and the inability to ask for explanation, I
struggled with losing control of my body. Many times I was
unconscious of the shift; many others, I was conscious of a
beautiful light intensifying within me and the cellular sermons
that followed.

At times, like my god-sisters, I was frustrated by the idea of
not controlling the way I spent my time. I had to become
accustomed to new foods, like *acarajé*, the bean pies sacred to
Iansá and *amalá*, the okra dish consecrated to Xango that I
now enjoy. In the beginning, my back ached and my fingers
cramped from long hours of sorting beans, chopping okra and
preparing shrimp for our public ceremonies attended by over a
hundred people. In the end, I grew to appreciate the medita-
tive cleansing repetition and stillness of it, in the loving company of my spiritual family.

Being American, it was assumed I did not know how to
wash clothes and sweep the floors. There were stereotypes
about privilege that did not mesh with my reality as a native
of the South Bronx and Harlem. In the beginning, I had few
intimate conversations with my god-mother, but she and I
grew to talking hours in her kitchen as she cooked my favorite
dishes. She threw a birthday party for me (during my first
birthday away from my twin sister) and supported me in my
other work-related projects in Bahia. My respect and love for
her has deepened over the years as our relationship has grown.
In my house, I have been at once an outsider and a daughter,
at times on the border of understanding and being understood,
but also loved, intimately known and generously provided for.

Another major challenge has been distance. To this day, I
wonder why it was Brazil, so far away, where I was called to
Oxum, and not New York City. What do you do when your
spirit finds a home that it has been seeking and you have to

leave it behind? After initiation, I had believed that somehow I would be able to remain tied to my spiritual community in the same intensity as I did while I lived in Brazil, but it has not been the case. The short two-week trips I am able to make now in no way compare to the experience of living there and attending the full cycle of spiritual ceremonies of my *terreiro*. Returning home to New York, I felt like I had lost a vital part of myself. I became disillusioned that something that had become an intrinsic part of my life had been reduced to five-day visits once or twice a year. A whole world that had opened to me was now only available in my dreams, brief visits and my own individual devotions.

I am learning that living with these mysteries is also a part of my path as a medium. My function is to be led, to be an instrument, a bridge, to surrender to the spirit, not to control or analyze it. To trust. I walk now, not always in understanding, but in faith, knowing I am kept and guided. On whatever side of the Atlantic I find myself, I know Oxum is walking with me. In her love, healing, creativity, beauty and sensuality —in the mirror of Her river—I see a glimpse of my own possibilities and the gifts she has passed on to me. It is an uncommon healing and communion, and when I can, I cherish the visits I am able to make to attend one of my *terreiro*'s *festas*.

Last year, the first of three trips back to Brazil, I returned for the *festa de* Xangô, the first in our cycle of almost ten public ceremonies during the year. The night before the *festa*, my god-sisters and god-brothers, the *ekedis*, *ogans* and *abians*[1] began the food preparations, talking, laughing, gossiping until eventually we spread our *esteiras* (straw mats) on the floor of

---

[1] *Irmão* and *irmão-do-santo*: god-sister and god-brother (initiates of the same god-mother); *ekedi*: a woman who does not receive the *orixá*, but cares for the initiated *terriero* members when their *orixás* arrive through trance; *ogan*: male leaders of a *terreiro* with special ritual and financial responsibilities, also seen as protectors of the community.

the *barracão*[2]. Some thirty or forty of us set up our bedding in huddles of four or five, and we drifted off, amidst giggles and snores, to sleep.

At four in the morning, the head *ekedi* woke us gently tapping, as is custom, on the soles of our feet. The roosters outside crowed in monotone and the house began to stir. We bathed and dressed in our *ropa da roção*, usually cotton skirts, an embroidered white camisole, wrapping our upper bodies in wide cloth tied with another thin piece of fabric. Most of the morning was spent attending to sacred ritual duties, prayers and obligations. Later we decorated the *barracão* in Xangô's colors and then performed the careful task of ironing and preparing our intricately sewn clothes, braiding each other's hair, borrowing each other's earrings, perfume and bobby-pins. It was time for a second bath, and then the lengthy process of getting dressed for the *festa*.

This time, I am one of some thirty-five women who file into the *barracão*. This time, I will dance. Slowly, the line moves forward as we sing for Exû, owner of the crossroads. One by one, we salute our head priestess, the *iyalorixá*, and our elders. Now I know the steps by heart, my bare feet move in step with my sisters. As the drum patterns change, their rhythms are familiar to me and I know the *orixás* they correspond to. The atmosphere is one of somber introspection and reverence, but inside I cannot stop smiling. It feels good to be back home to my spiritual house, however briefly.

II. POMPA: A Trans-Atlantic Freedom Route

Candomblé endowed me with spiritual resources to be an intermediary in another capacity, as co-founder and director of POMPA in Bahia. I served as a bridge between the Afro-

---

[2] *Barracão*: the public area of a *terreiro* where major ceremonies are held; also a principle collective space shared by members of the *terreiro*.

Brazilian and African American movements for racial equality, between Brazil's excluded youth and its most elite public institutions, and between the dreams of these youth and their creation of a new reality.

I launched POMPA during a Fulbright fellowship in Bahia, in partnership with the Steve Biko Cultural Institute. The Biko Institute, founded in 1992, is one of the premier college prep programs for Afro-descendent youths in Brazil. To date, the institute has placed more than 800 students in Salvador's public and private colleges. More than 2,000 youths have participated in the Institute's additional science and technology, human rights, professional development and community service programs.

POMPA's mission is to prepare low-income Afro-Brazilian college students for careers in public service and social entrepreneurship. Its vision is to build the capacity of Afro-Brazilian youth to be effective advocates for their communities and to increase the number of Afro-Brazilian professionals in Salvador's public sector. At its founding, POMPA moved beyond the predominant goal of affirmative action advocacy in Brazil for getting Black students into universities, to thinking of the opportunities needed after graduation.

The program was created because of the severe crises facing Afro-Brazilians, particularly youths. Brazil has the second-largest Black population in the world. Salvador da Bahia, one of Brazil's oldest, largest and poorest cities, has the highest percentage of Afro-Brazilians in Brazil. Despite their numerical majority, Afro-Brazilians consistently occupy the lowest positions in national indicators of income, health, literacy, housing quality, mortality and education. Two-thirds of all Afro-Brazilians live below the poverty line. Fewer than seven percent of all public-elected officials in Brazil are Afro-Brazilian. Only five percent of the 1.4 million students, admitted to universities in Brazil at the time when the program was launched, were

Afro-Brazilians. On average, Afro-Brazilians earn less than 40 percent of the salary of their white counterparts, and are 5.3 percent less likely than whites to be employed in professional occupations.[4] In his acceptance speech in 2001, Brazilian Finance Minister Antônio Palocci made an historic declaration that, "In Brazil, poverty has a color and an age. It is black and young."

Despite common knowledge of these problems, little was being done to reverse the exclusion of Black youth from the city's power structure. In the early part of my 2003 research, I asked the question, "How are Black youth being prepared for leadership positions in their communities and country?" In response, I often heard many outbursts of laughter, with the emphatic reply, "They aren't!" My field work revealed that there was a serious gap in the opportunities offered to teenagers and young adults. The majority of programs focused on engaging youth through arts and culture, but offered limited income-earning potential. Few programs offered opportunities for entry into professional careers in the public or private sectors, and especially not into leadership or management positions in those careers. Many of the youth programs in Salvador were meeting important service provision needs, but there seemed to be no model that would make a sustainable change in the distribution of power and wealth in this majority-black city.

At the time, I was already teaching at Biko, and volunteering as an organizational development consultant. I began talking with staff and students to learn more about the issues they faced. Several months into my research, I introduced a model based on my experiences in U.S. leadership programs. We worked together to adapt it to a Brazilian context, and POMPA was born. We joke that POMPA had an African American mother and Brazilian fathers: Biko's director, Silvio

---

[4] Sources: IBGE (Instituto Brasileiro de Geográfia e Estátisticas), DIEESE (Intersindical de Estaáística e Estudos Sócio-Econômicos) and UNICEF.

Humberto, and Durval Azevedo, POMPA's assistant coordinator. It was a family affair, at once successful, challenging and life-changing for us all.

POMPA students are typically residents of Salvador's poorest, most violent neighborhoods, whose families earn an average of U.S.$ 2,034 a year. In spite of tremendous obstacles, they have managed to become part of the first significant generation of Afro-Brazilian college students in the country. POMPA's pilot-year students were in various semesters of study in college, from freshman to senior. They represented a diversity of majors, such as law, business, international relations, journalism, engineering and others. Qualitatively, these students represented the vanguard of Salvador's young leaders.

Before POMPA's first anniversary, eight of twenty-one students were offered permanent positions in the organizations where they interned, such as the Municipal Secretary of Environmental Resources, the State Legislative Assembly of Bahia, the Municipal Secretary of Education, the Clemento Mariani Foundation, local television station TVE Bahia and several not-for-profit organizations. Of the eight students offered full-time jobs after their internships, at least three doubled their salary or that of their families, typically moving from 1-2 minimum salaries to between 3-5 minimum salaries. Several others have launched their own organizations as a result of their POMPA experience and are laying the groundwork to form their own not-for-profit organizations or local businesses. Two students are currently on POMPA's core administrative team, working with POMPA's second class, which is funded in part by the Kellogg Foundation.

Two years after its launch, POMPA has proven to be an effective and unique strategy for youth empowerment in Brazil. POMPA's site visits in Salvador and Brasilia gave our students a chance to enter and engage with institutions that have traditionally excluded Black youths. POMPA's curriculum offers students a unique look at issues affecting their community, increases their understanding of Brazil's domestic and foreign policies, and raises their self-confidence. POMPA's Internship Program is the first-ever internship program routing Afro-Brazilian youths into jobs in the city's key public and private institutions. Before POMPA, Black leaders in Bahia's political, legal, business and media fields had no formal mechanism to mentor Afro-Brazilian youth as to their professional goals.

What many students perceived as most important was that at POMPA they were asked for the first time in their lives "What do you dream?" and then they were given the resources to make those dreams a reality. "I always knew we needed to have more Afro-Brazilians in the state assembly, but I never knew it could be me," said one student. Based on their final evaluation forms, 80 percent of the students said that POMPA had "significantly changed their personal and professional trajectories."

In spite of our achievements during that pilot year, POMPA's path has also been full of public, administrative and personal challenges.

Public reaction to the program was overwhelmingly positive. POMPA was cited in some fourteen Brazilian media outlets its pilot year, including three national newspapers. In the community and among public sector leaders, POMPA students were regarded as an exceptional group of young leaders. The program itself was widely supported. We did, however, face criticism from some members of the Black movement because of our focus on institutional integration and on a population that was already privileged in many eyes: college students. In public and private conversations, I emphasized my belief that as a car needs more than one wheel to move forward, so Black people need a diversity of tactics to achieve socioeconomic equality; POMPA was only one in many worthwhile strategies. We debated about having the students wear suits, having them work in "the master's house, to learn the master's tools." We debated about the promise and the peril of integration in the African American and Afro-Brazilian contexts. There was never any real resolution, and at times I stood on both sides of the debate. What was most important was that the dialogue took place and that it continues.

The majority of our challenges came as a bi-national administrative team. Since POMPA is the creation of Brazilian and American partners, specifically the leaders and youths of the Steve Biko Institute and myself, we often needed to make adjustments for each other's different work rhythms, strategies and expectations. This international "marriage" is what makes POMPA so unique, but it is also our greatest difficulty. For example, I wanted to cap the class size at fifteen students, the number I had raised money for; they wanted twenty-one, a number that signified blessing in Afro-Brazilian culture, even though they had no new prospects for funds. I emphasized strategy, and they maintained the importance of also relying on intuition in our planning sessions. I thought we should also include the private sector as a route for student jobs, and they were opposed. I was meticulous about program evaluation, and they were not as reliant on strict measurements like "key metrics." I wanted to dock the students if they turned in late assignments without a formal excuse, while they argued that it was unjust, given the students' financial status. But we both believed that black youths should have a greater voice and place in Brazilian society and be trained to hold strategic leadership positions to advocate for their communities' rights. Standing on this fundamental understanding, having a profound respect for each other and knowing how to have fun in the process, enabled us to work together successfully.

On a personal level as the program director and principle fundraiser that first year, I pushed to meet the expectations of American donors, Brazilian partners and our students, leading a staff entirely in Portuguese. My friends, especially my boyfriend at the time, were concerned about the level of attention I gave POMPA, warning, "You are not POMPA, you are its founder, but it is not you. It is only a part of who you are." I moved between exhilaration and exhaustion frequently in the course of the day.

This was the greatest professional challenge of my life, mostly because my heart was sewn so deeply into it, but I was constantly aware that I did not work alone. Beyond the camaraderie and solidarity of my Brazilian team, I understood and felt the presence of my *orixás* and my ancestors. Even during the most intense days, I was able to give all I had to give, and then a lot more I didn't even know I had. The spiritual energy that surrounded me was like a great pool that I was diving in, a beautiful force that constantly revived and strengthened me. I knew that my capacity to run this program, and to stand at that middle ground, was a gift from my ancestors. I grew to understand, as they ministered to me, that I had been recruited to play my own small part to build on their work in forging a path to freedom for my own generation. The awareness of this accompaniment, as I worked, was one of the greatest blessings I received. I was working through a strength that was not my own, a force beyond me that opened the path for POMPA to progress.

POMPA has itself overcome the public, administrative and personal challenges it faced. According to Dr. Silvio Humberto Passos, Biko's Executive Director,

POMPA has opened an important and ample space for Afro-Diasporic collaboration. We've had the opportunity to live and practice the Afro-Brazilian and African American way to manage people, resources and the imponderable. Our partnership is marked by unity of action, planning, flexibility, intuition and also objectivity, creativity, commitment and the capacity to overcome obstacles. The result has been very successful: an unforgettable experience for all involved, principally our 21 POMPA students whose horizons were broadened, whose posture was changed, whose self-esteem was raised and whose commitment to their community was strengthened.

The program is now led completely by a Brazilian staff. I am moving onto another phase in my professional life, but continue to travel to Brazil to teach the flagship seminar on leadership and public management. I still keep in touch with the students and staff via email and just recently heard from a second-year student named Suéde that POMPA has been a "divisor das águas," a dividing water between "the life she had and the life she wants to create for herself and her community."

III. Implications for Diaspora Daughters

The stories I shared above about my experiences with POMPA and *candomblé* represent only one thread of a communal narrative about our identities and capacities as Black women of the Americas: as mediums between cultures, identities, freedom movements and spiritual planes.

My five years in Brazil blessed, stretched, tested and changed me profoundly. Up until a month ago, I had been unable to process it all. I felt overwhelmed by all of my conflicting emotions. I missed my spiritual family, my friends, my POMPA students and team, my neighborhood, and the way of life I loved and had become accustomed to. Finally, one year after my return to New York, I can make some sense of it all. In stillness, the lessons have made themselves clear.

Standing at the crossroads is both a privileged and precarious position. You run the risk of being crushed in the collision of communities, identities, responsibilities, self and spirit. In embracing one world, you may lose your ties to another. In fact, you could lose connection with your own self. Those who learn to master the middle, however, have an insight to give each of the roads that meet in them. The vantage point, at the middle, is clairvoyant. It is a place of creativity, innovation, negotiation and transformation. It is the place where weakness becomes strength, where impossibility becomes possibility, and where your vulnerability opens you to unfathomable power.

Standing at the crossroads requires great humility and also great self-confidence. As a medium or intermediary, you are only a channel; you are the means but not the end. Yet, you also have to believe in your abilities, your own worth and your own sight in the midst of the intersecting worlds. You cannot get lost in translation. This requires balance. It requires rest. It requires love. It requires deep reservoirs of faith. It requires community. It requires a belief in and knowledge of your destiny. It requires a belief in the indestructibility of your soul.

This is how you survive. This is how you walk your part of the road between the ancestors and the children. This is how you live out the meaning of your birth.

In Brazil, some days I felt stranded in the traffic jam of worlds and identities, and on others my passage was clear and powerful. Directing POMPA, the intersections of race, nation, language, sex, class and political ideology collided within me. At my best, however, I was able to pull the common threads together to help create a new strategy that is slowly changing the balance of racial and generational power in the city. The precise reason that POMPA worked was because it was born at the crossroads. It was created in the intersections of the American and Brazilian conceptions of race and anti-racist strategies, being led by a woman on an all-male team in a male-dominated society, directing a team in a language that was not my mother tongue, advocating for institutional integration in the midst of a movement that favored grassroots organizing strategies and standing at a place of privilege in the midst of great poverty. The meeting of Brazilian, African, Caribbean and African American ancestors in my life imparted me with strength, insight and energy to do this. On the path leading to my initiation in *candomblé*, the limits of my physical body, mind and faith were tested in ways they never had been, but I received and became a conduit for a power I had never known with such intensity. I received access to resources, to healing and to guidance that enabled me to fulfill a vital part of my destiny and, in my own small way, that of our people.

What inspires me now? A deep and proven knowledge of the crossroads power. It is available wherever identities and spiritual planes intersect. I thrive in the middle ground; I love the bridge role, even as I navigate its difficult and unpredictable contours. Brazil taught me the most about this power that springs from the place where the horizontal line of the Atlantic Ocean meets the ladder between heaven and earth, connecting the ancestors to the youth. I believe that is where the greatest power is concentrated. I believe it needs to be nurtured in order for us all to be healed, to truly achieve mental, spiritual and socioeconomic freedom.

I invest my energy at both ends of the bridge. In the spiritual, I pay homage to God, to my ancestors and to my *orixás* with *ebos* (offerings) of prayer, song, food and ritual attention. I am grateful for their enabling power in my life, and I feed it as it feeds me. In the secular world, I turn my attention always to our children. I believe young Black women in particular have a special capacity that needs to be nurtured. Youth and women have a strong capacity to be mediums because of their natural proximity to the spiritual world. The added ancestral inheritance of Africa deepens that capacity. It is coded in the DNA of all young Black women, but they often do not know how to access it.

Too often, the youngest Diaspora daughters get caught in the crossfire of tongues, color, dollars, sex and green cards; they never get to know their own power. They often lack the tools to negotiate a life out of poverty, self-hatred, sexism, racism and xenophobia. The right tools can come from secular and spiritual education, from love and community. They come from domestic and international policies that promote equality of resources, voice and opportunity. These tools also come from sharing our collective stories.

Over the past fifteen years, I have often focused on the secular education of young women (and men), helping to provide training in basic education, community organizing, policy advocacy and professional development.

These days, I am more concerned with spiritual education. I have learned that when a woman is aligned with her spirit, she is like a river flowing, able to surpass any obstacle, any border. This doesn't mean that everyone must get initiated or even practice an African religion, but there are ways to teach anyone to touch, know and cultivate their own spirit, their own life force, and that is the most important work for our future. Spiritual power enables all other power.

Certain principles from the religion can equip diaspora-daughters to fulfill their full potential, such as the concept of *iwa pele* (good character), the *roda*, (ring of community) in which everyone has an important place and role; the value for personal responsibility and hard work; the mentoring relationship between *adoxós* and their *mãe-pequenas* ("little mothers": a practice of pairing an older god-sister with a new initiate as a source of support and instruction). There is the idea of the *benção*, which like the Sanskrit greeting *namaste* acknowledges the divinity in each of us and also symbolizes respect for our elders. An important concept is that each person has a special *caminho* or destiny to fulfill in life, and how to align with that path. They need to know about the *axé*, the spiritual power, they possess, which is the creative, life-giving power of God. Of all these, it is most important that Diaspora daughters receive the knowledge that they never walk alone. They need to know that each person has a spiritual force within them and surrounding them that they can access for guidance, comfort and protection. These are the lessons we need to pass on to young women as strategies for wholeness, fulfillment and freedom. These tools give us resources to deal with the trauma of being black and female in the Americas. They give us power to resist injustice. They inform our ability to create something new out of nothing, just as they did for our foremothers and forefathers.

In many ways, the dreams of youth are a continuation of the ancestors' dreams and desires. It has always been youth—with the presence of the ancestors known or unknown—at the helm of the world's most powerful freedom movements. As it was in Soweto and Selma, it is now in Salvador da Bahia. Young people, unlike most adults, have the energy, time, candor, faith and will required for resistance and social change, if they are properly trained. That is our job and it awaits us in urgency, on whatever side of the Atlantic we live.

Editors

Marta Moreno Vega is a professor at El Centro de Estudios Avanzados Puertorriqueños de Puerto Rico y El Caribe in San Juan, Puerto Rico; she has also taught at Hunter College, City University of New York. She authored *The Altar of My Soul* (One World/Ballantine, 2001) and *When the Spirits Dance Mambo: Growing Up Nuyorican in El Barrio* (Three Rivers Press, 2002). Also, she is the founder/president of the Caribbean Cultural Center African Diaspora and co-founder of the Global Afro-Latino and Caribbean Initiative. She lives and works in New York City.

Marinieves Alba is a Puerto Rican/Panamanian activist, producer and writer, who has worked in the arts, and youth and community development throughout the United States and Latin America for over 15 years. She has dedicated her life to exploring and nurturing the intersections between the arts, social justice and issues of social and cultural rights and equity for Puerto Ricans, Latinos and other people of color in the United States. She has focused on cultivating attention solidarity, inter-cultural understanding and collaboration between Afro-Latinos and other peoples of the African dias-

pora. Marinieves holds degrees from Wesleyan University and
New York University's Wagner Graduate School of Public
Service, and is a graduate of the NALAC Arts Leadership
Institute and the Third World Newsreel. Currently, she is a
citizen journalist/correspondent for World Pulse/Pulsewire, a
women's communication network dedicated to connecting
women and social change work globally and Community
School Director in Washington Heights, New York.

Yvette Modestin, a writer and activist focusing on Afro-
Latino issues, was born and raised in Colón, Panama. She is
the founder/director of Encuentro Diaspora Afro in Boston,
Massachusetts, which mobilizes the Afro-Latino community,
empowers young girls of African descent and builds bridges of
understanding between African Americans and Latinos. She
is currently the Diaspora/Canada Coordinator of the Red/
Network de Mujeres AfroLatinoamericanas, Afrocaribeñas y
de la Diáspora. Yvette has been profiled by the *Boston Globe* as
"The Uniter" for her work in bringing Latin American and
African American communities together and for her activism
in building a voice for the Afro-Latino Community. In 2006,
she was highlighted as "Six in the City" by the *Boston Globe*
for her service in the community. She continues to address
race in the Latino community and to increase awareness of the
Afro-Latino/a experience.

Contributors

Nirva Rosa Camacho Parra is a psychologist, leader of the Afrodescendent Women's Network and Director of the Cumbe de Mujeres Afrovenezolanas.

Shirley Campbell is a renowned Costa Rican poet, writer and and anthropologist.

Mónica Carillo is an Afro-Peruvian Hip-Hop activist, writer, poet, singer, musician, community leader, journalist, human rights advocate, feminist and educator who works to empower her community, especially younger generations of Peruvians who live under poverty.

Ana-Maurine Lara is an award-winning novelist, playwright and poet. She is working on a Ph.D. in African American Studies/Anthropology at Yale University.

Evelyne Laurent-Perrault was born and raised in Venezuela by Haitian and Venezuelan parents. Evelyne studied, lived and traveled through Europe, Africa, Latin America, North America and the Caribbean. Evelyne has a B.S. in Biology from the Central de Venezuela and is a Ph.D. candidate at New York

University in the History Department's African Diaspora program in Latin America and the Caribbean. She organized the first Arturo Schomburg Symposium at Taller Puertorriqueño.

Diva Moreira is a political scientist who has been involved in social movements since the 1960s. She founded Casa Dandara, a cultural center promoting black self-esteem and leadership, for which she was awarded an Ashoka Fellowship. She has been a visiting scholar at the University of Austin, Texas, as well as at The Wilson Center in Washington D.C., where she conducted research comparing race relations in the United States and Brazil. Since leaving the United Nations Development Program in Brazil, she has been working as an independent consultant on issues of politics and social equality. She was recognized by City administration (or by the Mayor) of Belo Horizonte as a member of the Council for the Promotion of Racial Equality.

Vânia Penha-Lopes, Ph.D., is professor of sociology at Bloomfield College and co-chair of the Columbia University Seminar on Brazil. A native of Rio de Janeiro, Brazil, she focuses her research and teaching on comparative race relations, family, gender and social stratification.

María I. Reinat-Pumarejo is co-director of ilé: Organizers for Consciousness-in-Action (formerly Institute for Latino Empowerment), an organization committed to anti-oppression organizing in Puerto Rico and the United States, which she co-founded in 1992. María is also a Core Trainer with The People's Institute for Survival and Beyond, based in New Orleans, L.A., and is an influential member of the national multi-racial network of anti-racism organizers.

Ana Irma Rivera Lassén is a feminist activist, lawyer and defender of human rights, particularly of women, people of African descent and LGBT-identified people. She co-founded several important organizations in Puerto Rico on these issues and is internationally recognized as a specialist on these topics. She is a professor, essayist, short story writer and poet.

Marielba Torres, Ph.D., Centro de Estudios Avanzados de Puerto Rico y el Caribe, San Juan, Puerto Rico has published several essays at the national and international level. She is a researcher, writer, faculty and cultural facilitator.

Lorelei Williams serves as Programs Consultant for Project People Foundation. She launched PPF's *South Africa Grant Fund* and managed the *Uniforms 101* and *Crafting Social Change* projects. Lorelei has worked for the last fifteen years to empower youth throughout the African Diaspora, including the United States, South Africa and Brazil. In 2003, she earned a Fulbright to Brazil where she founded POMPA, a leadership development program, to train Afro-Brazilian college students for public service careers. In addition to her work with youth, Lorelei has also been a Production Editor for the Harvard *Journal of African American Public Policy* and interned at the White House and the South African Parliament. She currently works as a consultant for organizations such as the Ford Foundation, Brazil Foundation, The Brazilian Institute of Ethnic Media and others.